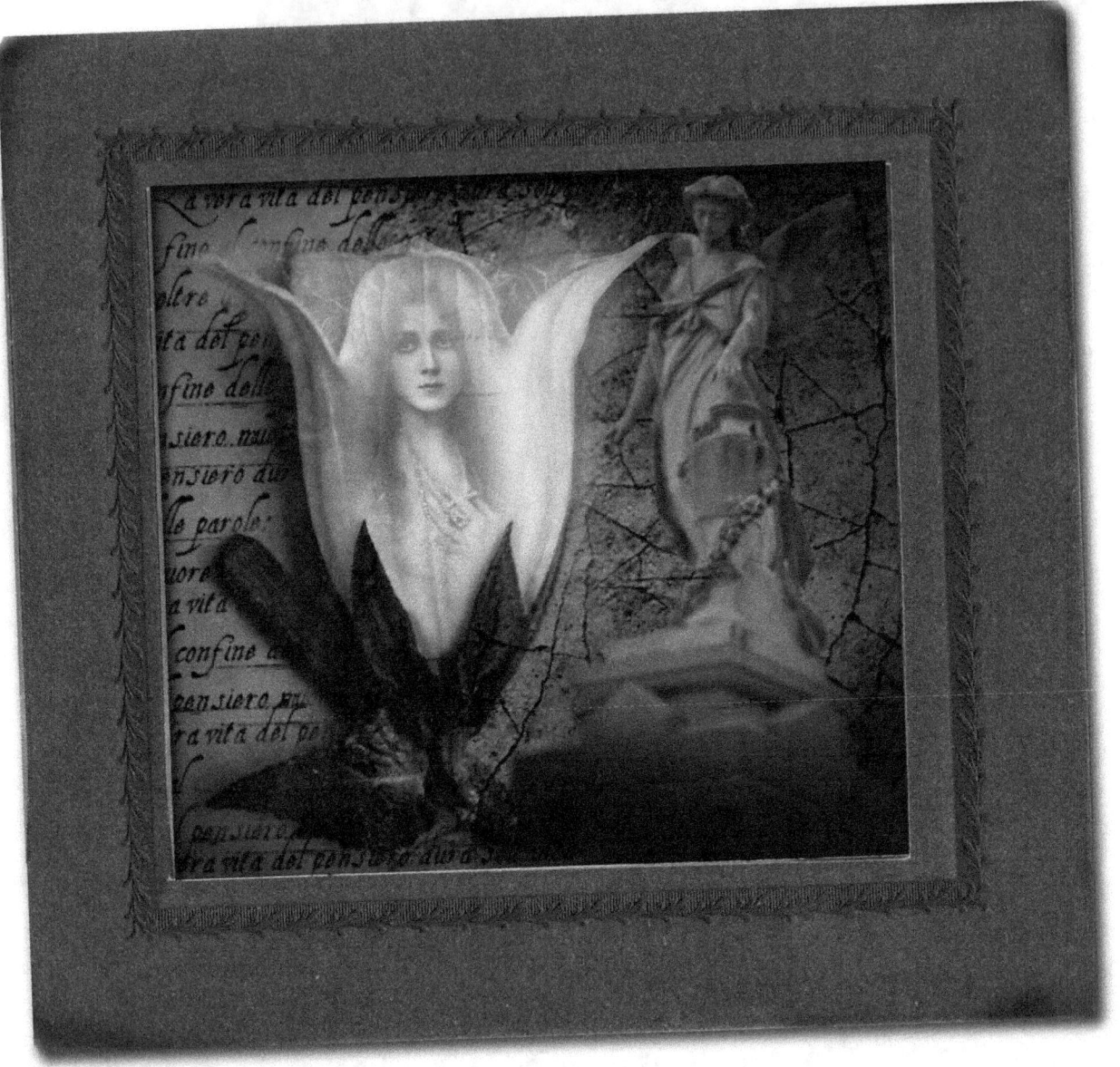

Deadly Nightshade by Lisa Vollrath

The day which we fear as our last
is but the birthday of eternity.

--- Lucius Annaeus Seneca

Artists
in This Issue

Jennifer Minnis lives in the San Francisco Bay area, and works primarily in mixed media and book arts. She cuts intricate traditional paper cuttings (scherenschnitte), binds books, alters anything in sight, and even created her own imaginary country, Albanlea, to write about and illustrate with her art. More of Jen's work can be seen on her web site at www.jenminis.com.

Marian Savill lives in Cambridgeshire in the East Anglia region of the UK. Her mixed-media work includes altered books and other forms of altered art, artist trading cards, mail art, art journals, collage and decos. Marian's work can be seen in her art blog at theartfulzebra.blogspot.com.

Diane Ferguson lives in the Houston area, and in addition to her mixed-media work, is an accomplished weaver and fabric artist. Her art can be seen in her blog at soonerorlater.blogspirit.com.

Lisa Vollrath is a prolific mixed-media artist. Her work covers a multitude of techniques, from altered books to collage, from artist trading cards and decos to textile art and costume design. She has written dozens of books and how-to articles for arts and crafts publishers. Her current work can always been seen on her ever-growing web site, LisaVollrath.com.

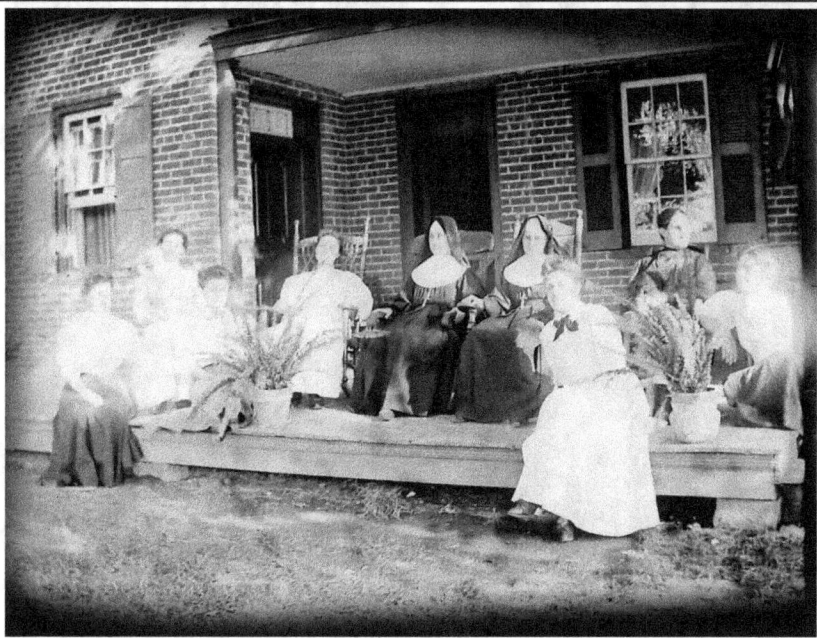

A Few Words From Lisa

It's been two years since I've published an issue of Bad Influence. A lot has changed in my life since the previous issue...

I'm out on my own now, instead of working for other people. It's both liberating and completely terrifying. I have complete freedom to do whatever I like, whenever I like. I also have to ensure that the bank account is fed regularly---so if whatever I like strays too far from what's popular at the moment, I'm taking a big risk.

Having said that, when I started planning this month's issue, there was really only one choice for a theme, and I thought it probably wouldn't be popular: I wanted to write about photographing cemeteries, decaying buildings, and the historical obsession people seem to have with those things. I was certain this zine wouldn't sell many issues---and equally certain that if I didn't write it, I'd never be able to move on to another theme.

Big surprise. Pre-orders for this zine blew my socks off, and when I put out a quiet call for photography, hands went up on both sides of the ocean. This issue includes photos by artists Marian Savill, Diane Ferguson, and Jennifer Minnis, and is my first tentative step toward creating a publication that represents many artists. I'm getting tired of just writing about my own work---I'd like to talk about some other people for a change!

So, here it is: issue #2. Here's hoping that issue #3 doesn't take me another two years to put together...

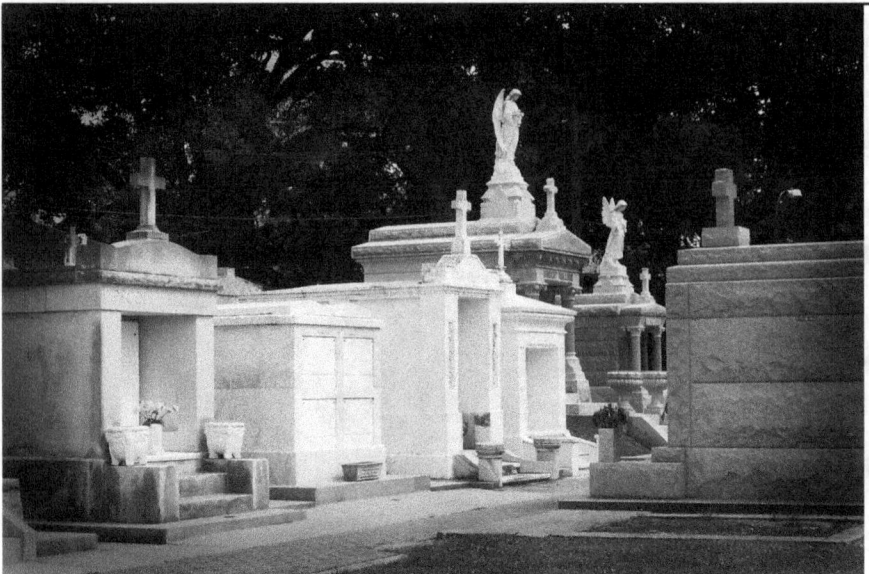

Cemetery Photography

I've been photographing cemeteries for about ten years. I think it started one afternoon when a friend and I were driving around in the country, looking for old buildings to shoot, and came upon an old cemetery. It was pretty and green, and the grounds had lovely light. What photographer could resist? Ever since, I've spent a little time each season exploring old cemeteries, working on my photography skills.

Whenever I get the urge to shoot some cemetary photos, I don't have far to go. There are many small historical cemeteries in the area where I live, which is a little surprising, since I live in an urban area. It's hard to remember that even though it's wall to wall city in the Dallas-Fort Worth metroplex, most of what's here was built relatively recently. A lot of what is developed now was rural farmland fifty years ago. That's true of many cities, so if you're looking for a place to shoot your own photos, you may not have far to look for a suitable spot. There are many listings of small, old cemeteries online, posted by gene-alogists---just do a search of your city or county and state.

I'm constantly surprised when I pull up in front of a cemetery I've read about online, only to discover I've driven by it a hundred times. I've discussed this with other cemetery photographers, and it seems to be a common phenom-ena. Perhaps we've conditioned ourselves not to see them---and maybe that's a good thing, because many of the small historical ceme-teries I visit have a somewhat un-touched look to them.

I generally shoot photos with a friend. This is partly for the shar-ing aspect---it's nice to speak to someone who is also interested in photography in hushed tones about what I'm seeing, or how to solve difficulties in composition. It's also for safety. As I said, small historical cemeteries tend to be areas that most people overlook. They're usually fairly empty in my neck of the woods, even on Satur-day afternoon. While the solitude does mean I don't have to worry about someone tromping through my carefully framed shot, I've occa-sionally seen other people eyeing my photography partner and head-ing toward her---and then stop when they see me heading for her or hear me call her name. Perhaps they only wanted to strike up a conversation, or perhaps her very expensive camera caught their eye. Better safe---take a friend, and make sure you keep an eye on each other.

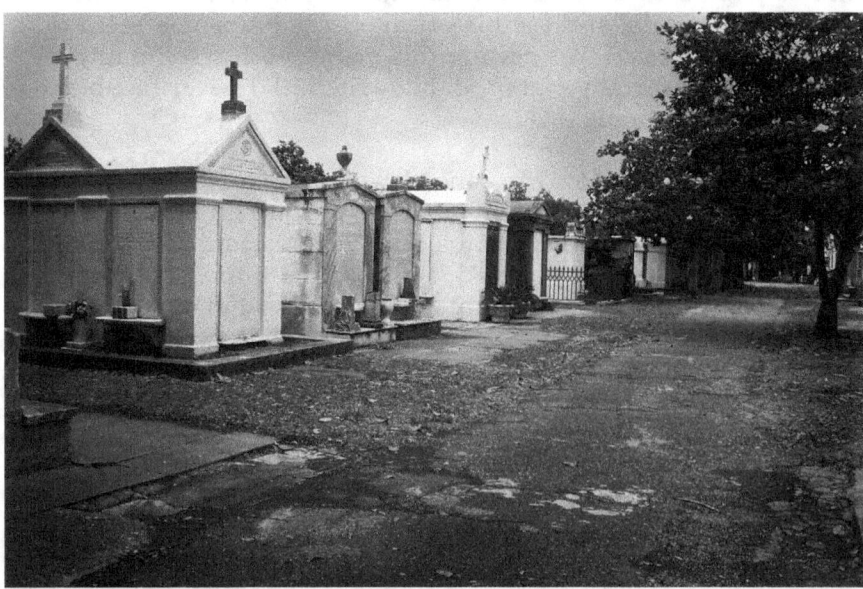

Below is a photo of photographer friend Robin Sowton, shooting the monument I captured in the two photos at right. Robin and I have learned to stay out of each other's way on photography outings, generally heading in opposite directions when we work in the same small cemetery. I always take at least one shot of Robin shooting something I've already photographed---not because she enjoys having her picture taken from this particular angle, but because it shows me later the big picture of what we were working with that day. Here, you can see the obstacles: a big telephone pole just to the right rear of the figure, lots of telephone lines, and some really overgrown crepe myrtle trees. Also, the sky that day was very clear and flat, with no clouds. This can be both a blessing and a curse: while the lack of clouds means no wrestling with extra shapes in the background, it can also make for large areas of blankness in finished photos. My solution: heavy work in PhotoShop.

The two photos at right have been enhanced in Photo-Shop. At top, I've manipulated the sky to add a little visual interest. Unfortunately, at this angle, I couldn't capture the figure's face. Moving around the monument to get a good shot of the face meant there would be power lines in my photo. These have been removed from the sky sections of the bottom right photo.

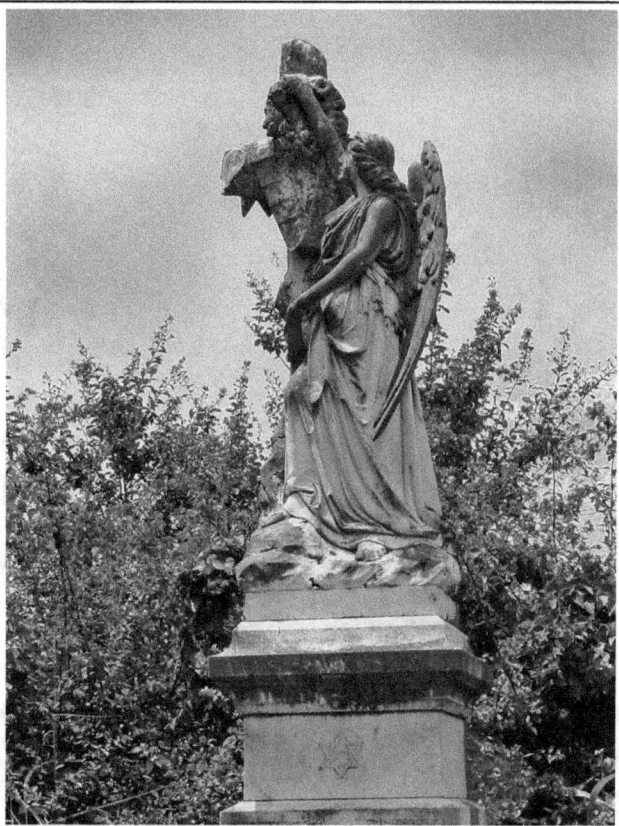

Photos on these pages by Lisa Vollrath.

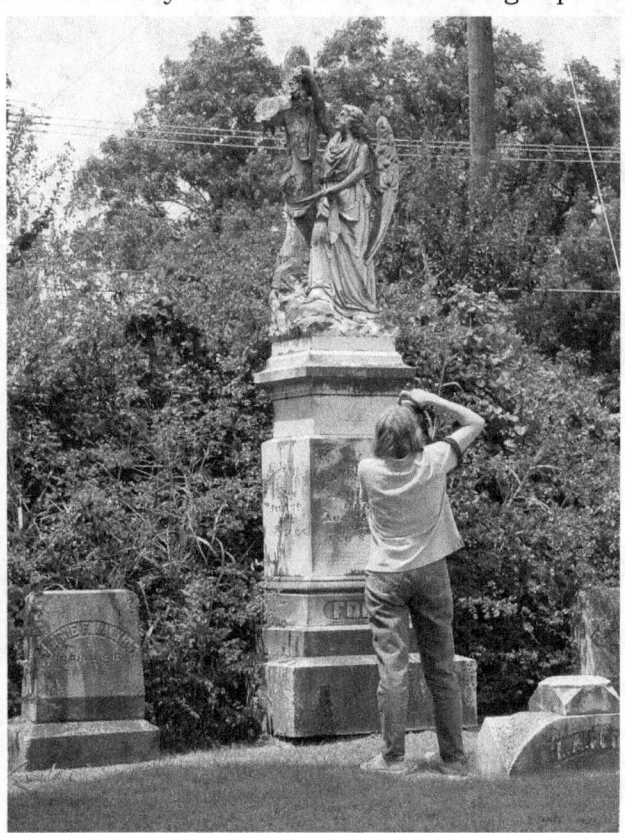

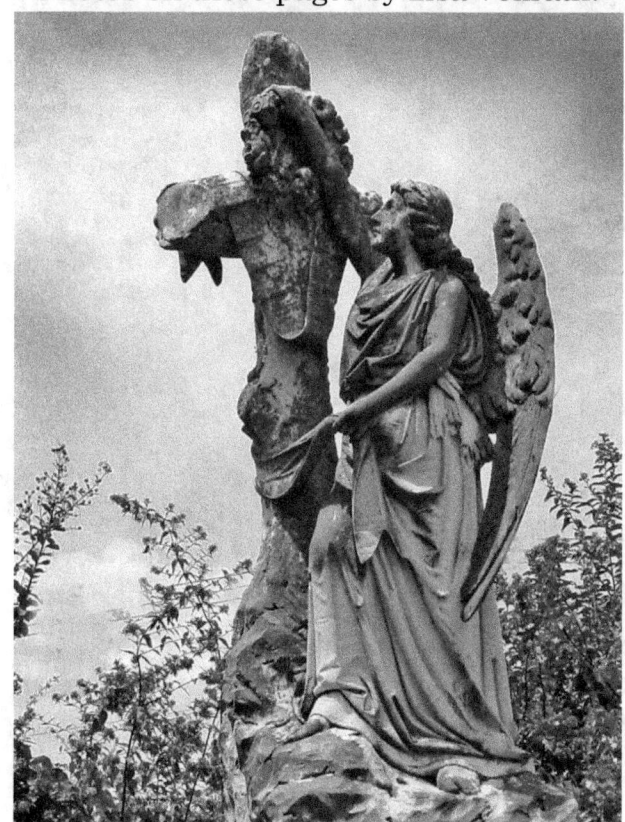

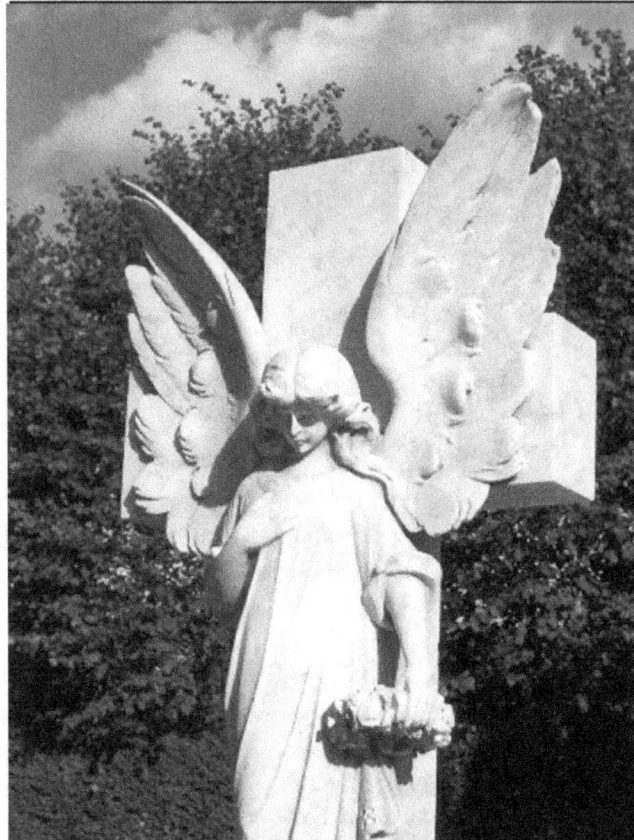

Cemetery Photography
by
Marian Savill

A few thoughts about the appeal of cemeteries from Marian:

"I love visiting cemeteries! I always find them peaceful and tranquil. There are many things that attract me to headstones - their agedness, the
colours, the shapes, the words and the lichens growing on them, so much waiting to be captured by sketch, painting, photograph or written word.
Every artist can find inspiration in a cemetery!"

"Every artist can find inspiration in a cemetery."

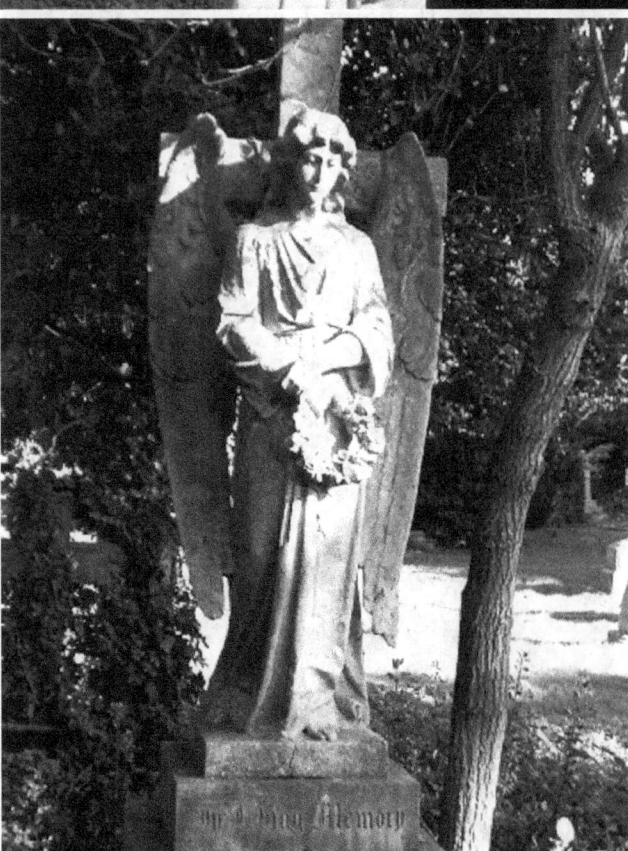

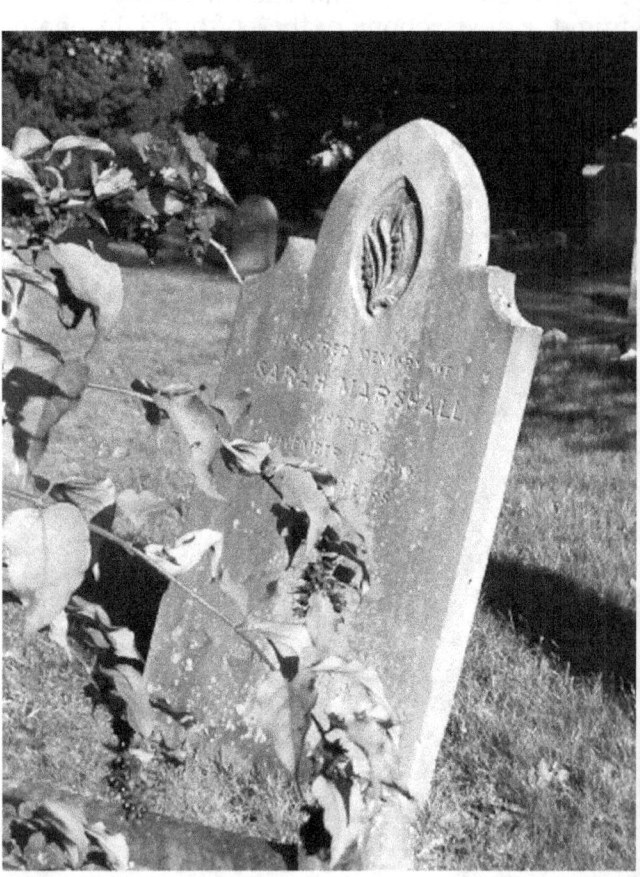

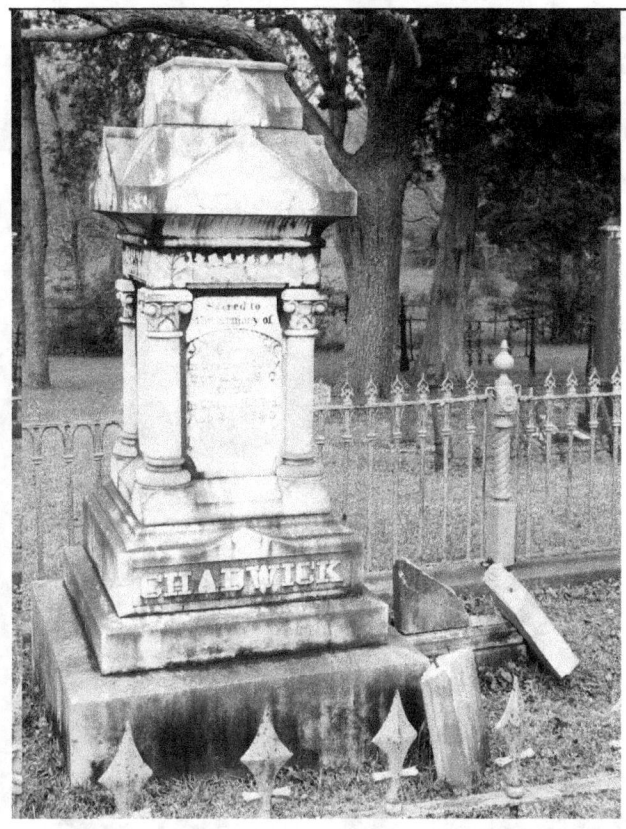

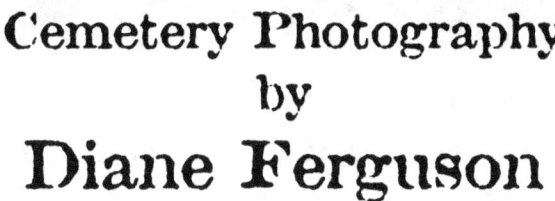

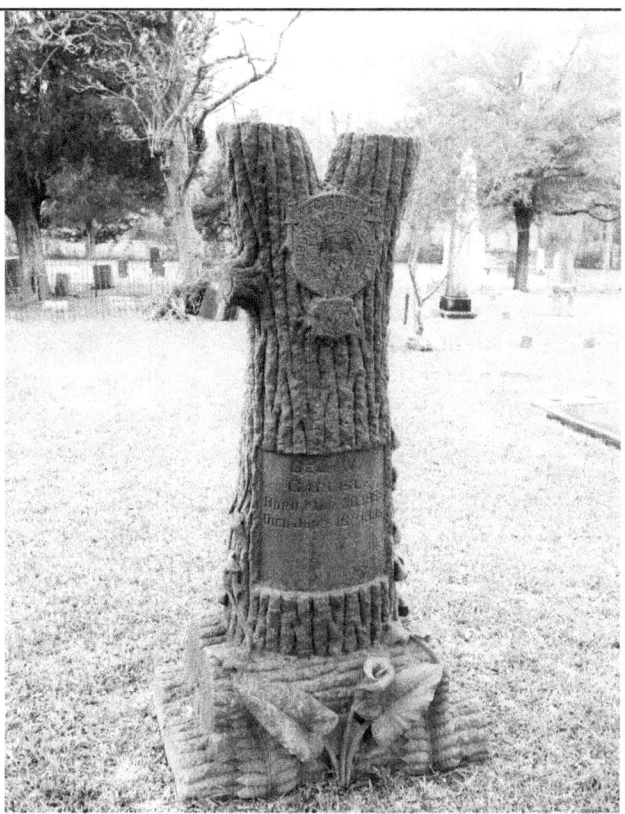

Cemetery Photography
by
Diane Ferguson

"I don't expect anyone to wander by a well-tended gravesite and see my name etched in stone."

A few thoughts from Diane:

"I do not wish to be buried beneath the earth, although I do find old headstones rather intriguing. These photos were taken in a Masonic cemetery in the hill country of Texas. The artwork involved in the carving of the stones impresses me, and the stone in the shape of the tree trunk makes an unusual statement. I am a tree hugger at heart, so if I was inclined to have a monument, I would chose a tree. However, I expect my ashes will be cast upon my garden if it is still in the family or mixed with the sand in the desert of Arizona. I don't expect anyone to wander by a well-tended gravesite and see my name etched in stone. I prefer to think of my spirit blowing in the wind. "

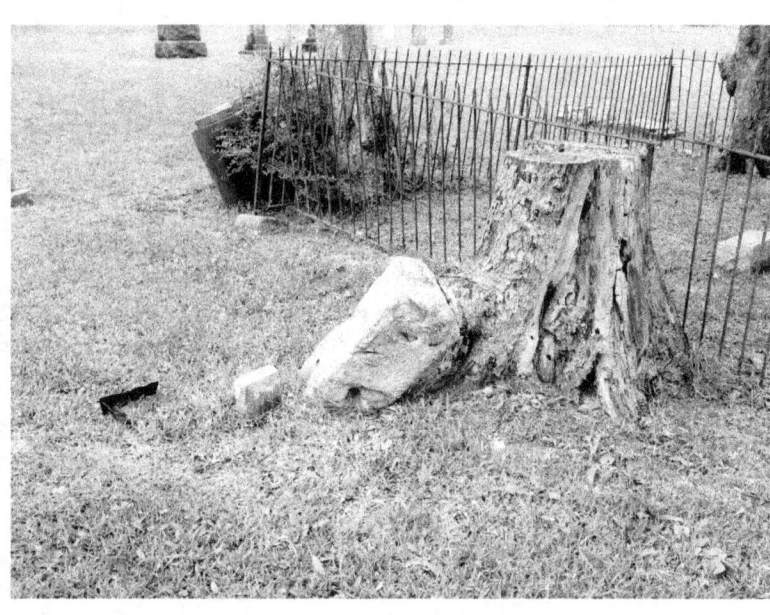

Cemetery Photography
by
Jennifer Minnis

I asked artist Jennifer Minnis to share some thoughts about cemetery photography:

"I love to go photo hunting in cemeteries because they're such serene places. For the same reason, I used to go on picnics in them when I was a teenager. They're a place of peace without all the hustle and stress of life. Because of this, it's possible to capture shots of beautifully aged and patinated stone and metal, or more classical styles of carvings... things that are rarely allowed to age naturally and still stand so pristine and respected elsewhere. These don't all have to be focused on death. Cemeteries are rather focused on death, naturally... but they are also places of beauty."

"When I'm out photo hunting in cemeteries, I am usually looking for either beautiful shots that stand alone, or elements that I can use in my artwork. I often draw from the designs I've photographed on old headstones for pen and ink drawing, or even soft block stamp carving. Sometimes I keep a photo record of stones I want to revisit at a future time to make rubbings from. I am working on a series of scherenschnitte paper cutting designs drawn from the wrought iron fence patterns that surround many of the really old plots in a couple of local historic cemeteries. "

"And, of course, there is always a use for them in collage and altered photography..."

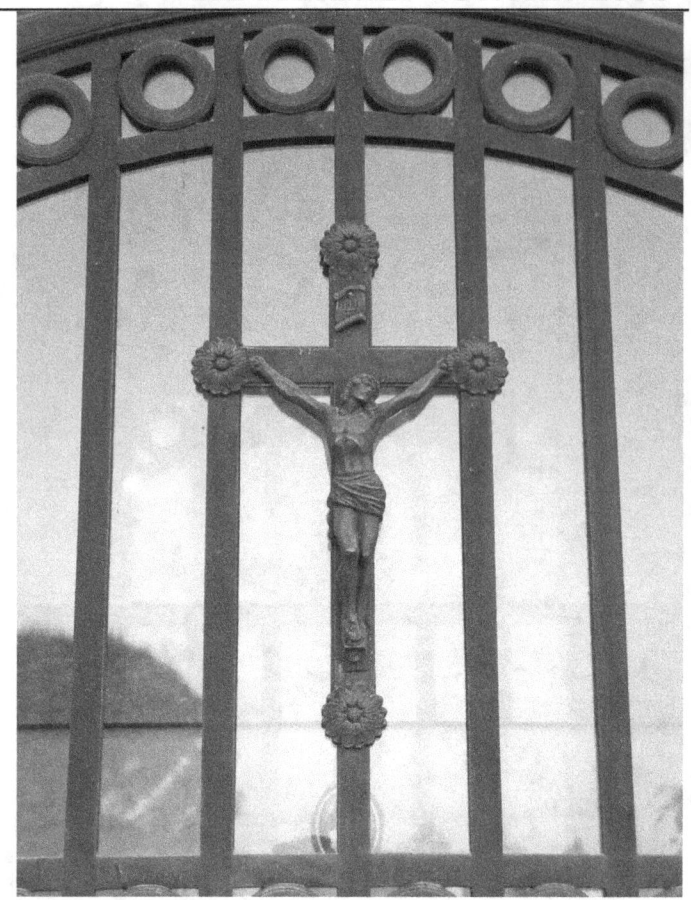

"Cemeteries are rather focused on death, naturally... but they are also places of beauty."

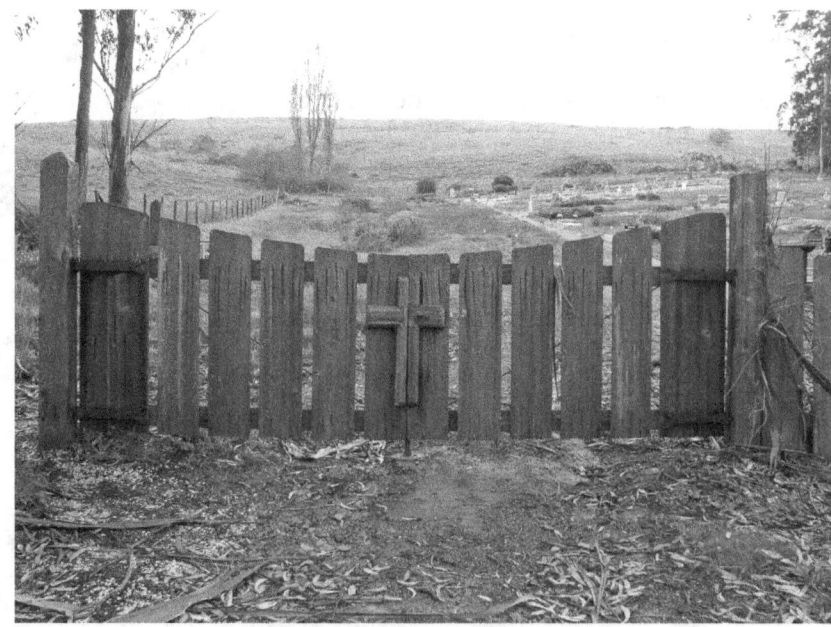

Tombstone Symbolism

Many of the old cemeteries in my area date from the mid-nineteenth century. Like many things from the Victorian era, tombstone decorations often contain symbolic meanings. These are some of the common ornaments and themes found on tombstones from the 1800s:

Anchor - Hope, or a seafaring profession.
Arrow - Mortality
Birds - Eternal life or resurrection.
Broken Column - The loss of the head of a family.
Broken Ring - The family circle has been severed.
Butterfly - Short-life or early death.
Corn - Ripe old age.
Crescent - The deceased was probably a Muslim.
Cross - Resurrection.
Crossed Swords - Military person of high rank.
Dove - Innocence or peace.
Fruits - Eternal plenty
Full-Blown Rose - Died in the prime of life
Garland - Saintliness and glory.
Hand Pointing Up - Pathway to heaven.
Hands Clasped - Farewells or marriage
Hands Praying - Asking God for eternal life.
Heart - Love.
Two Joined Hearts - Marriage.
Hourglass - Time has run out.
Ivy - Immortality, friendship.
Lamb= Innocence, grave of a child.
Lily - The virgin's flower, innocence and purity.
Menorah - An emblem of Judaism
Morning Glory - Beginning of life
Oak Leaves & Acorn - Maturity, ripe old age.
Open Book - Deceased teacher or minister.
Poppy - Eternal sleep.
Rosemary - Remembrance.
Sun - Renewed life.

There are also many symbols that have local meaning. For instance, there is a variation of the tree-shaped headstone Diane captured in one of her photos that is often seen in cemeteries about an hour north of me. That symbol was used to mark the graves of people associated with The Woodmen's Home, an home for widows and orphans in that area. The recurring use of the same grave marker caused me to do a little research, and come up with the association.

Keep an eye out for recurring symbols in your area, and see if you can connect them to events or organizations that were active during the times indicated on the grave markers that bear them.

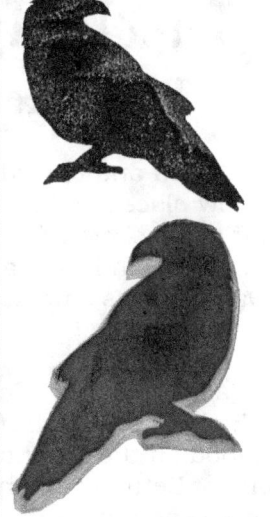

A Bird in the Hand

When Jennifer Minnis took the photo below, she captured a priceless moment---a large black bird in an interesting pose, perched atop a cemetery monument. Even though the raw photo presented the challenge of a less than ideal background, Jen saw the potential in various parts of this photo, which she has used in several pieces of artwork. She's cropped the bird to use alone on ATCs, and she also turned him into a hand-carved stamp, shown above. Good job, Jen!

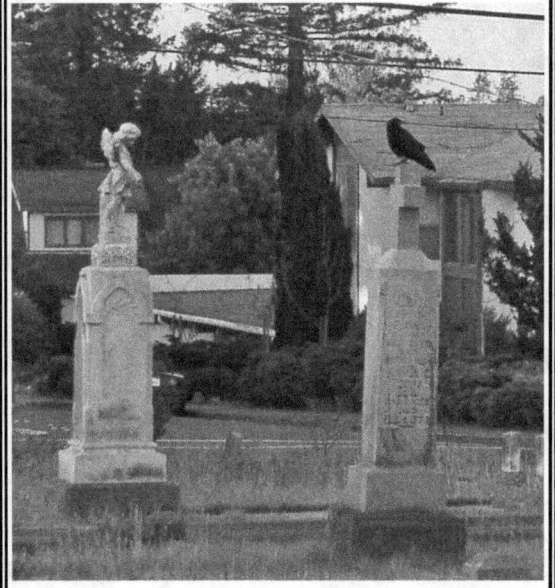

Photography by Jennifer Minnis

Little Hearts in a Row
The Six Robinson Children

One lovely spring day, Robin and I decided to get out and find some new places to photograph. I did a search online for small cemeteries close to her house in Plano, Texas, which is a heavily populated suburb of Dallas. I was surprised to find so many little places to explore!

Not far from Robin's place is Bethany Cemetery. It was founded in 1877, along with a church and school that originally stood on the grounds. While the other portions of Bethany of long since been razed, the cemetery is still in good shape, with many tombstones dating from the late 1800's.

Robin and I have a habit of going our separate ways when we photograph, keeping out of each other's shots by working opposite sides of the grounds in sort of a circle. If one of us sees something interesting, we'll flag the other down and point it out. Often, I see things that Robin, who is by far the better photographer, will enjoy shooting.

In the far corner of the cemetery, close to the street, and set away from most of the other headstones, I found a row of six heart-shaped stones. These stones are fairly common in this area, so I really didn't register at first what I was seeing. As I passed by each stone, inspecting them to see if they offered anything of interest, it suddenly hit me that the stones all bore the same last name. Upon further inspection, I discovered the six identical stones were for children from the same family. I did the math at each stone, and realized that none of them had lived much beyond a year--and most had died within months of birth.

Now, I'm sure we all learned in school how hard life was for folks who came West, and we've all heard statistics about how high infant mortality was in past centuries. Seeing these six tiny grave markers in a nice, neat row really drove that home for me. Some poor mother lost six babies in seven years---and almost 100 years later, here they are.

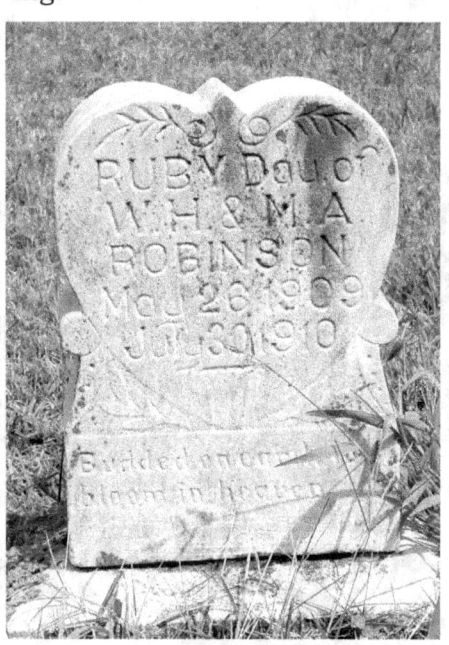

Ruby
Born - May 26, 1909
Died - July 30 1910
14 months

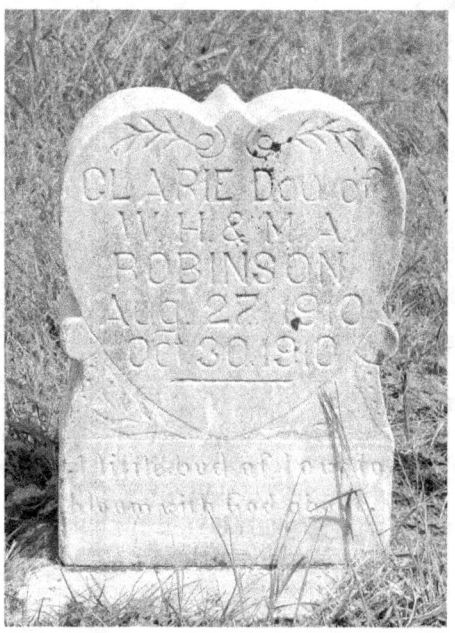

Claire
Born - August 27, 1910
Died - October 30 1910
2 months

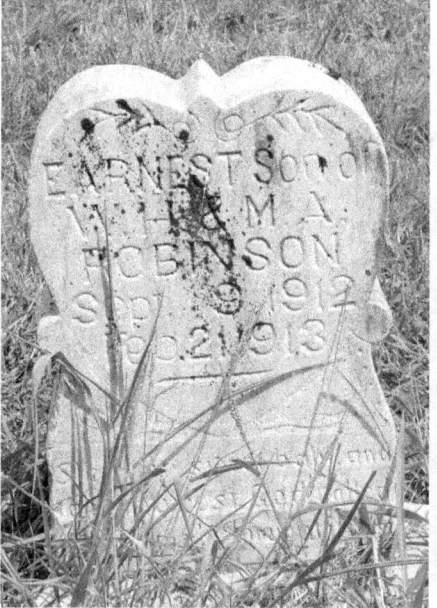

Earnest
Born - September 9, 1912
Died - February 21, 1913
5½ months

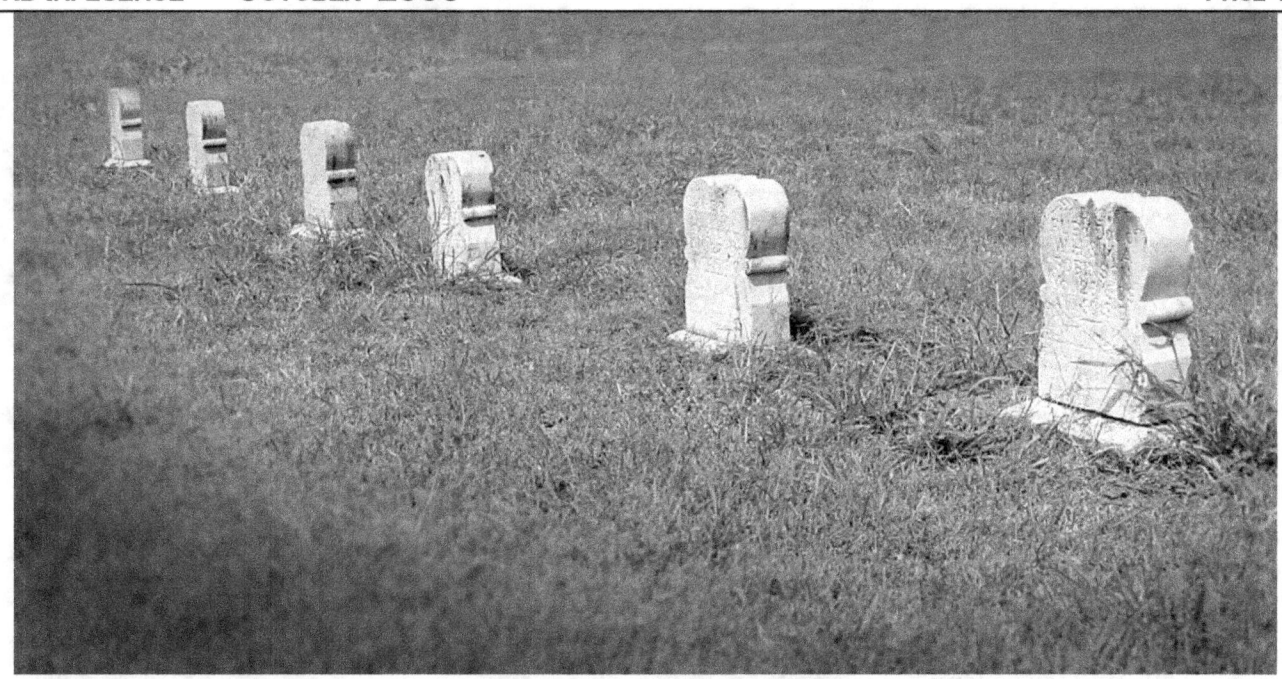

There are other Robinsons buried in the same cemetery, including William H. Robinson. Perhaps he was the father of these six? The dates on his stone indicate he would have been in his thirties when these children were born. His wife is also there---Myrtle O. Robinson. She also would have been in her thirties when these children were born. Could she be their mother? Or was she his second wife? The initials on the six little graves say M.A. Robinson. Where is she?

I'm often asked where I get ideas for my work. Wandering in this small cemetery, I had the tiny glimmer of an idea for a piece. Eventually, it grew into eight pages of an altered book.

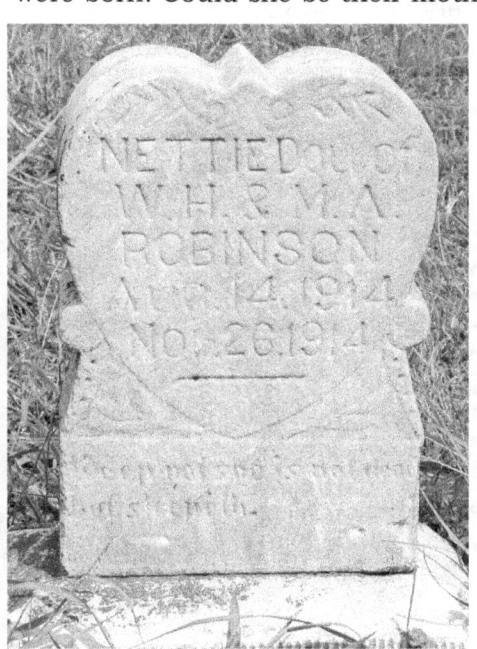

Nettie
Born - August 14, 1914
Died - November 26, 1914
3 months

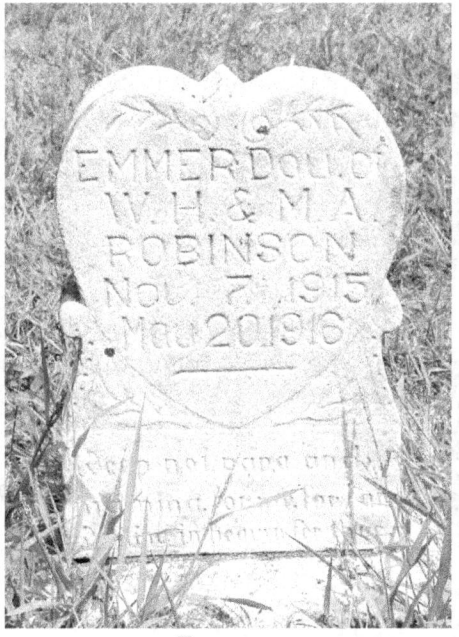

Emmer
Born - November 7, 1915
Died - May 20, 1916
6½ months

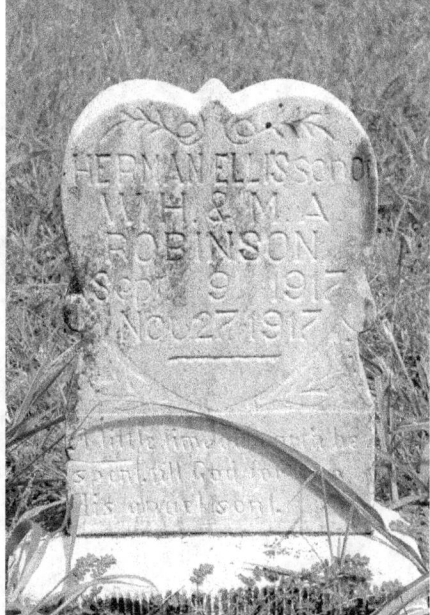

Herman Ellis
Born - September 9, 1917
Died - November 27, 1917
2½ months

I See Dead People
Victorian Post-Mortem Photography

Of all the odd items I've collected for my art, this one definitely raises the most eyebrows: I collect Victorian post-mortem images. No, not photos of autopsies---photos of people taken after they've passed on.

Popular photography began with the advent of the daguerreotype in the late 1830s. Although the process produced a very accurate image, it demanded precision and care. Subjects were required to remain perfectly still for as long as fifteen minutes. Naturally, healthy, happy children proved to be poor subjects for this type of photography---they simply couldn't remain still that long.

It's important to remember that in the Victorian era, death was very much a part of everyday life. Child mortality, in particu-

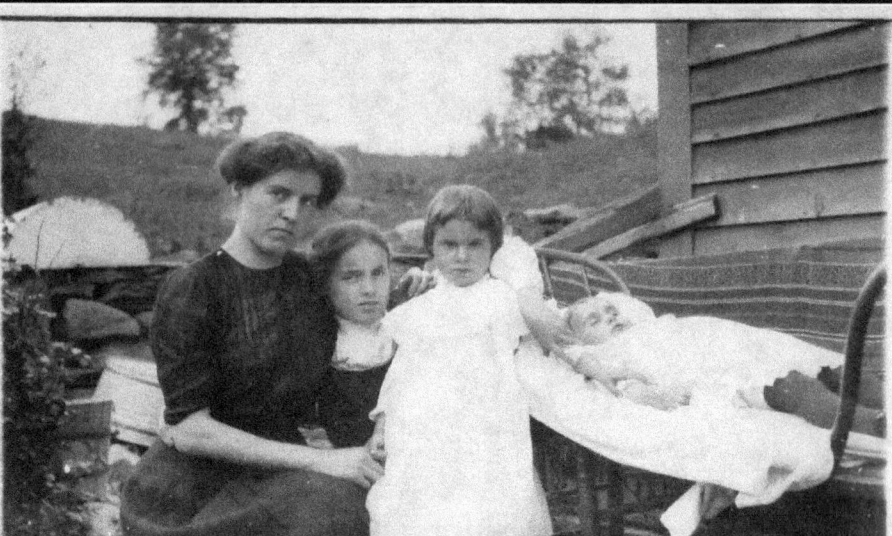

lar, was very high. Children were often lost before reaching their first birthday. The death rate came very close to matching the birth rate.

Put the advent of photography together with a high child mortality rate, add the fact that the likelihood of a photograph of a child being produced prior to death was very low, and you'll understand why post-mortem photos came into being. Very often, the photo taken after death was the only image a family might have of a loved one, particularly if that loved one was a child. This was the one and only remaining chance to have a photographic memento.

In many post-mortem photographs, the departed is captured as if peacefully asleep. While some post-mortem photos are taken in caskets, many more are taken with the deceased laid out on a bed or chaise, with a few personal items close by. Children might be surrounded by their toys, and young women might be dressed in their confirmation or wedding gowns. In many cases, very small children were photographed being held by a parent or sibling. Sometimes, entire families would gather around the departed to take a final family portrait with their loved one.

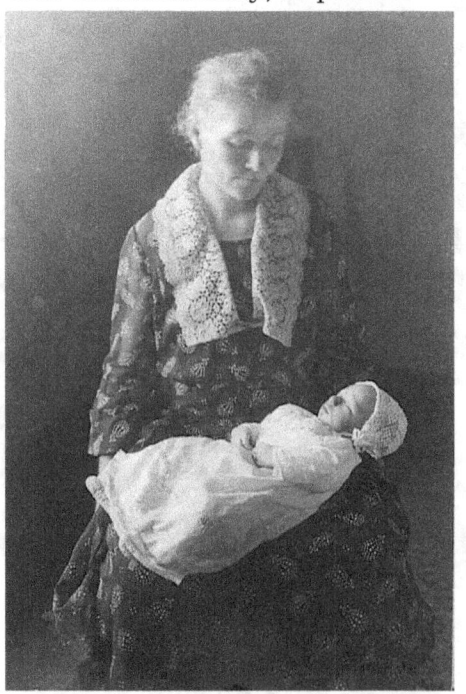

As photography progressed from daguerreotypes to ambrotypes to tintypes to the very inexpensively produced carte de visite, more and more people could afford to have photos taken. The carte de visite also offered for the first time the opportunity to produce multiple prints of the same image, so many copies of a post-mortem image could be made and sent to family members as a remembrance.

Sometime last year, I had the opportunity to purchase a CD filled

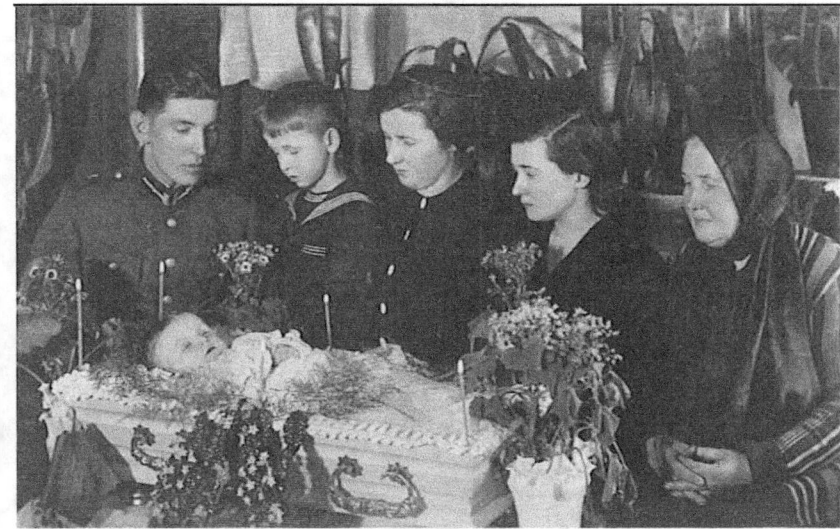

"What a comfort it is to possess the image of those who are removed from our sight."

Flora A Windeyer
in a letter to
Rev. John Blomfield,
November 1870

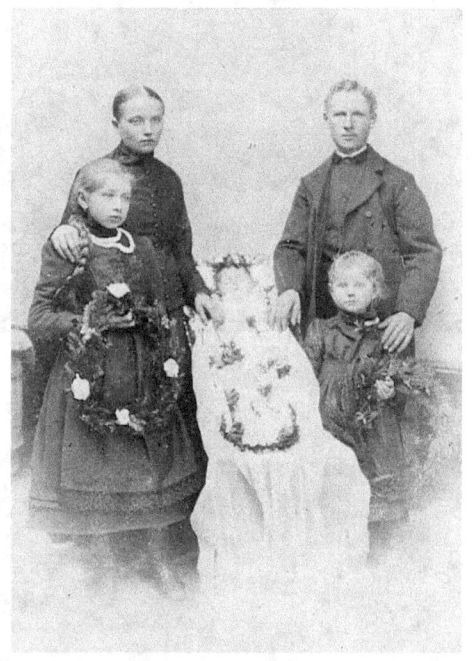

with scans of a very large collection of post-mortem photographs. These photos have become quite collectible over the years, and now fetch very high prices. I felt quite fortunate to obtain these images as a group, before they were auctioned off and separated. The photos on these pages are from this collection.

On the facing page: Bottom left - This CDV image from around 1914 is one of the most recent in the collection, and shows a typical pose of a mother holding her deceased child. Top right - A CDV from the early 1900s depicting a family whose youngest member has passed on. This photo is somewhat unusual in that it was taken outdoors at the family farm, in a somewhat casual pose.

On this page: Above - A final family portrait from 1930s Europe. Right - Another family portrait, circa 1860s America. Lower left - Mother and child circa early 1900 Pennsylvania. Lower right - This type of seated pose amongst family heirlooms was common for adults. Circa 1890s America.

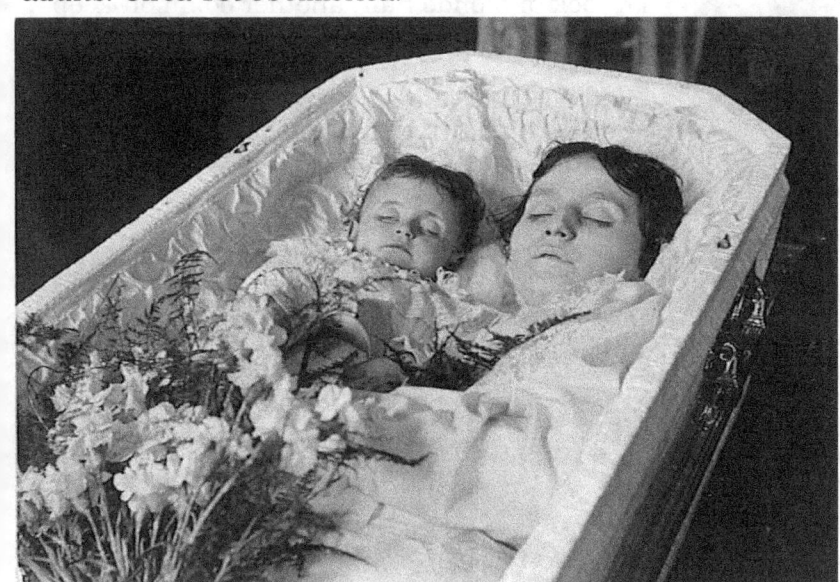

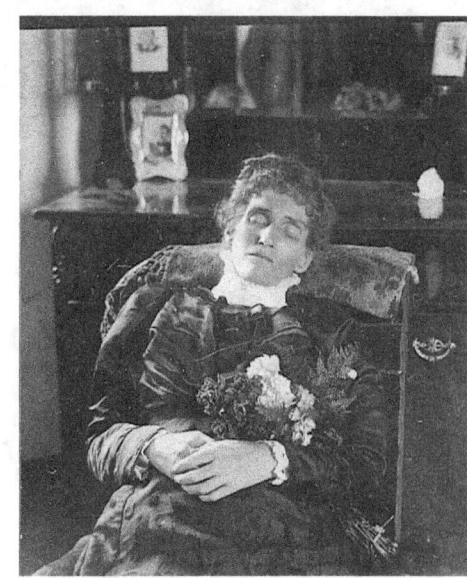

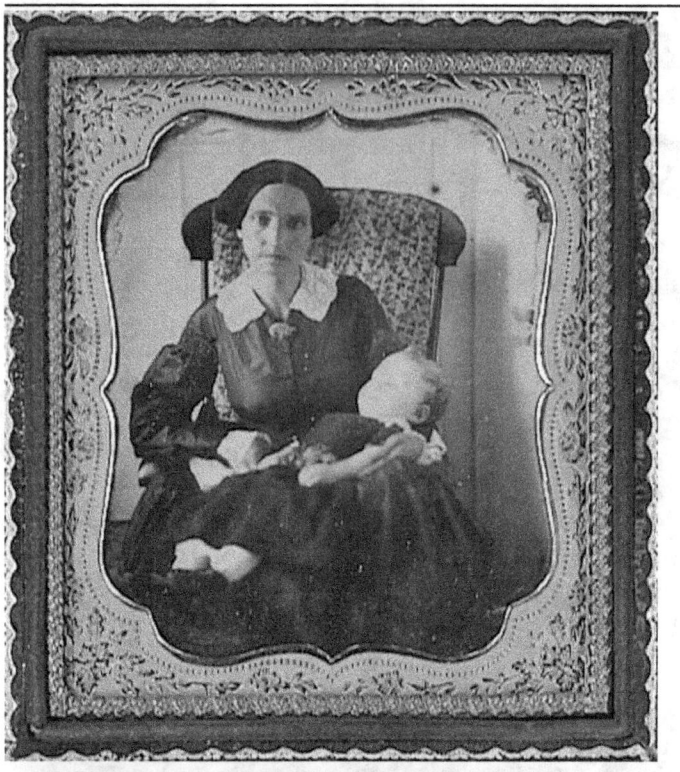

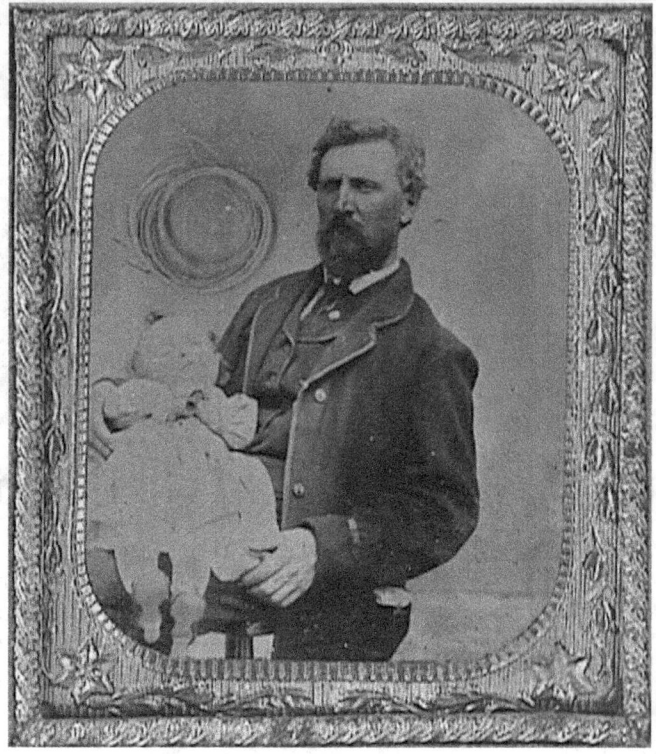

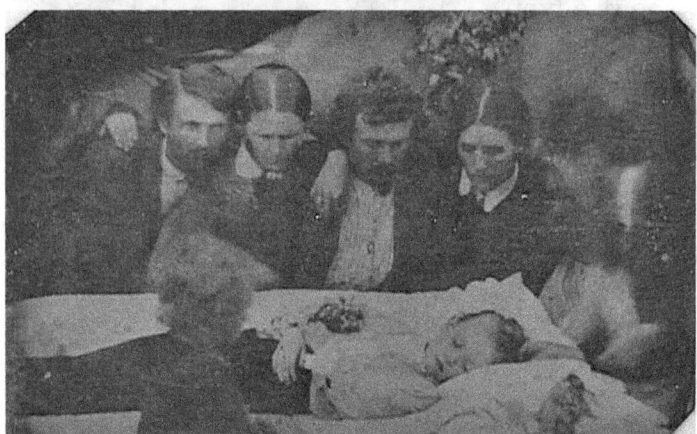

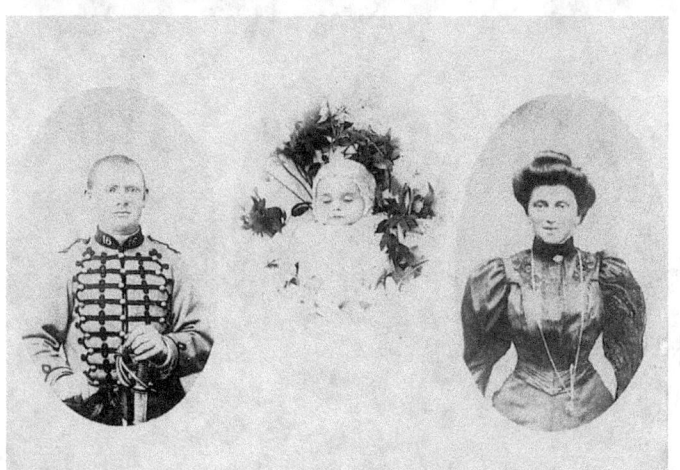

On this page:

Above left - A daguerreotype from the mid 1950s. Mothers are often shown holding their lost children in their laps, rather than cradled in their arms.

Above right - An ambrotype from the 1860s. Enclosed in the case with the image is a circular lock of blonde hair, another common keepsake.

Middle left - A family portrait tintype from the 1860s. The blurred figure at right is a man who moved during the process. This type of blurring is typical in early photos.

Lower left - An interesting family set from the 1890s. The three photos were clearly taken at three different times, cut out, and glued together to create a single CDV.

Putting It Together
Eight Pages from Dead Like Me

Although my goal with this issue of Bad Influence was to produce something that isn't my usual how-to thing, I do feel the need to tie everything back to making something. All roads lead to finished artwork...

So, how do cemetery photographs, Victorian most-mortem photos, and six tiny heart-shaped headstones turn into art? For me, they all came together in an altered book layout.

A while back, I agreed to do a local altered book project with a couple of folks who live close by. After tossing around a few themes for our project, we decided to center our books on death. Probably not your usual theme for an altered book round robin, but when all artists are so completely in agreement about a single theme, I take it as a sign.

My book was titled Dead Like Me, and I focused the work on specific events and people. For one section of the book, I decided to deal with the six Robinson children. I combined the photos of their headstones, my recently acquired collection of post-mortem photos, and my ever-growing file of cemetery shots into an eight page layout.

At right is the beginning of the section. I left the first and last pages their full width, and trimmed the center pages slightly narrower. The face of the little girl at far right is visible on all pages, and is the Robinson name at the far left.

So, here are seven headstone photos (I'll talk about number seven in just a bit), a blow up of the name Robinson, and a post-mortem shot of Mother, Father and a child who has passed on, along with a shot of an angel taken at a local cemetery.

Monday's child is fair of face.

Tuesday's child is full of grace.

Wednesday's child is full of woe.

Thursday's child has far to go.

Friday's child is loving and giving.

Saturday's child has to work for a living.

But the child who is born on the Sabbath day is fair and wise and good and gay.

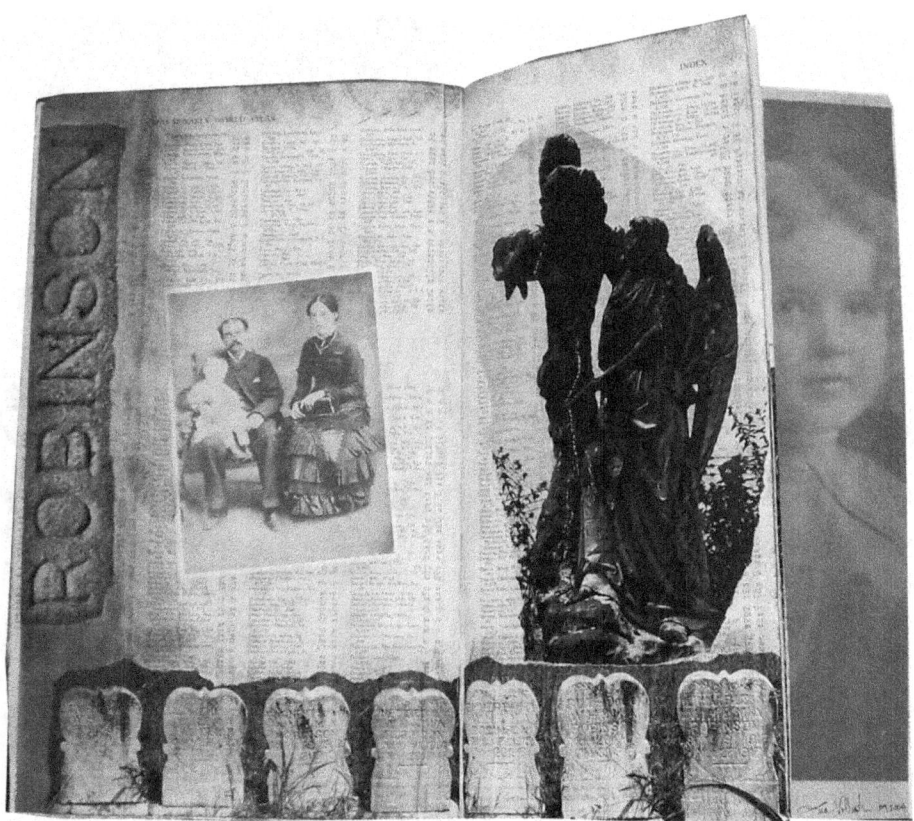

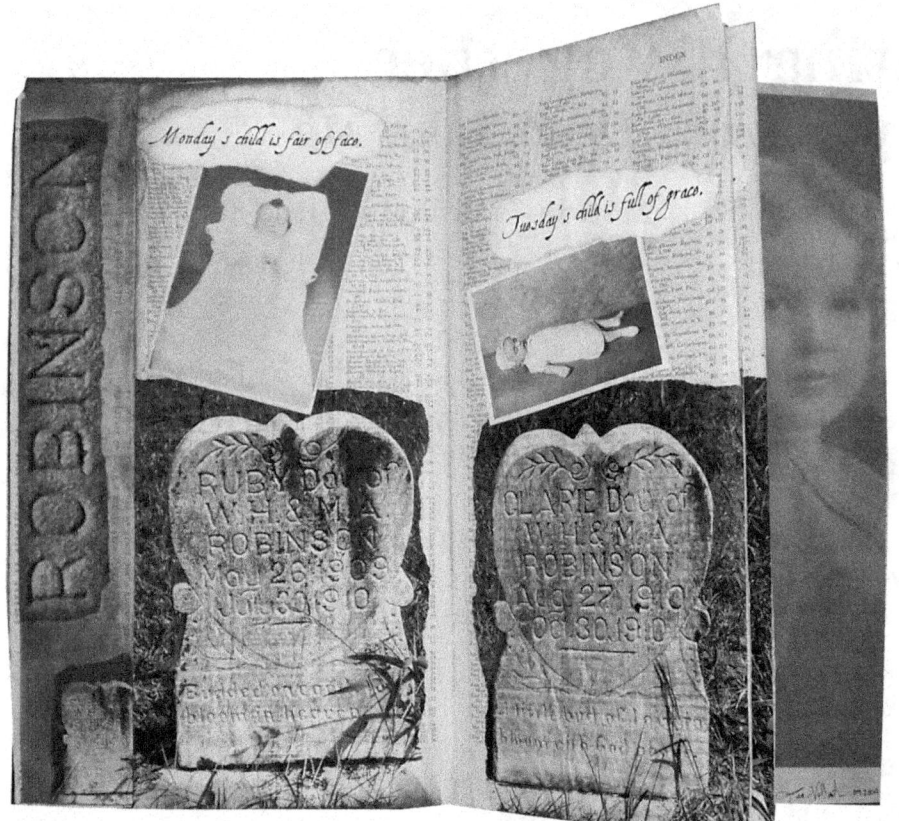

The interior pages of the layout each portray one of the Robinson children. I used a larger image if the individual headstones, and a post-mortem photo that roughly corresponded to the age of the child when he or she died.

Part of my inspiration for this layout came from the nursery rhyme on page 15. Each child represented a day of the week, so each page had one line of the poem on it.

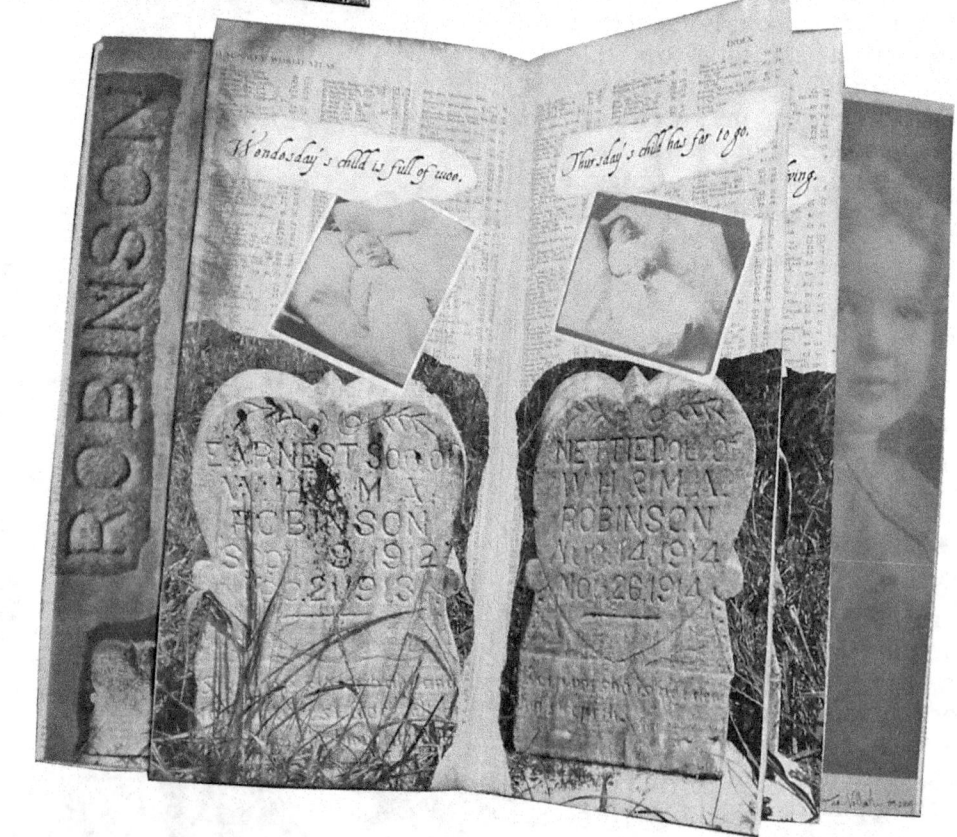

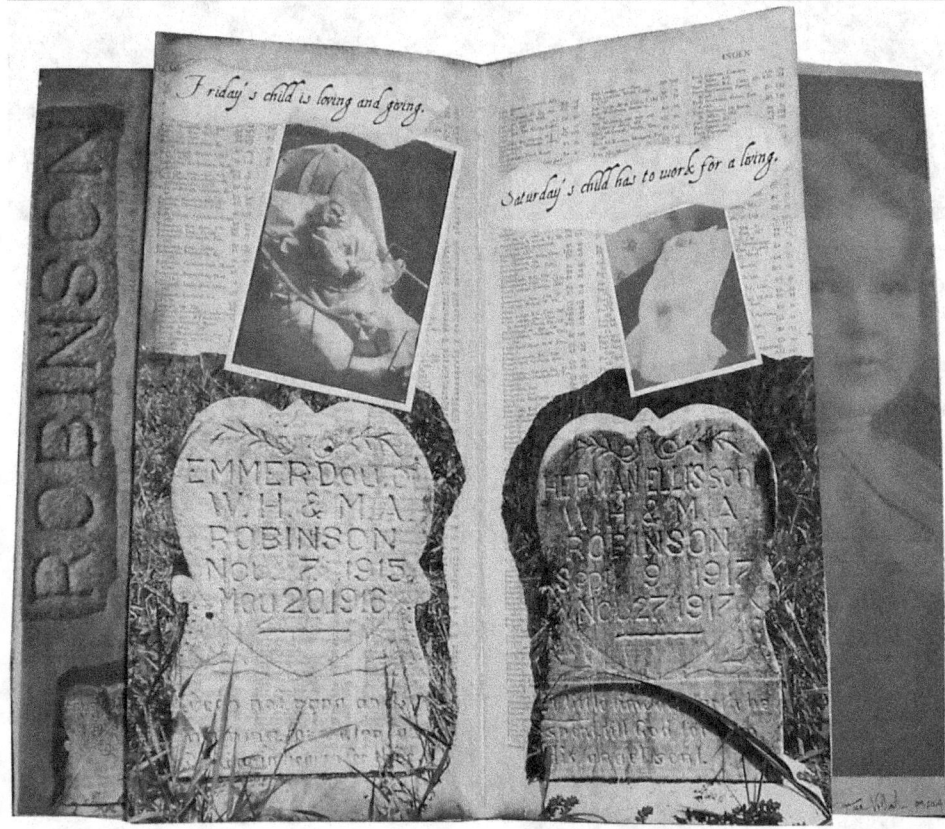

As the pages turn, the same to side sections remain visible, and the general layout of each page remains the same. The only things that change are the name on the headstone, the photo of the child, and the line of the poem.

I needed seven headstones to make this layout work, and I had a lovely photo of a slightly older child in my collection of post-mortems. She looked very much like the little girl shown on the right. I decided to do a little work in PhotoShop, and created a seventh headstone, for a sister who lived until she was ten.

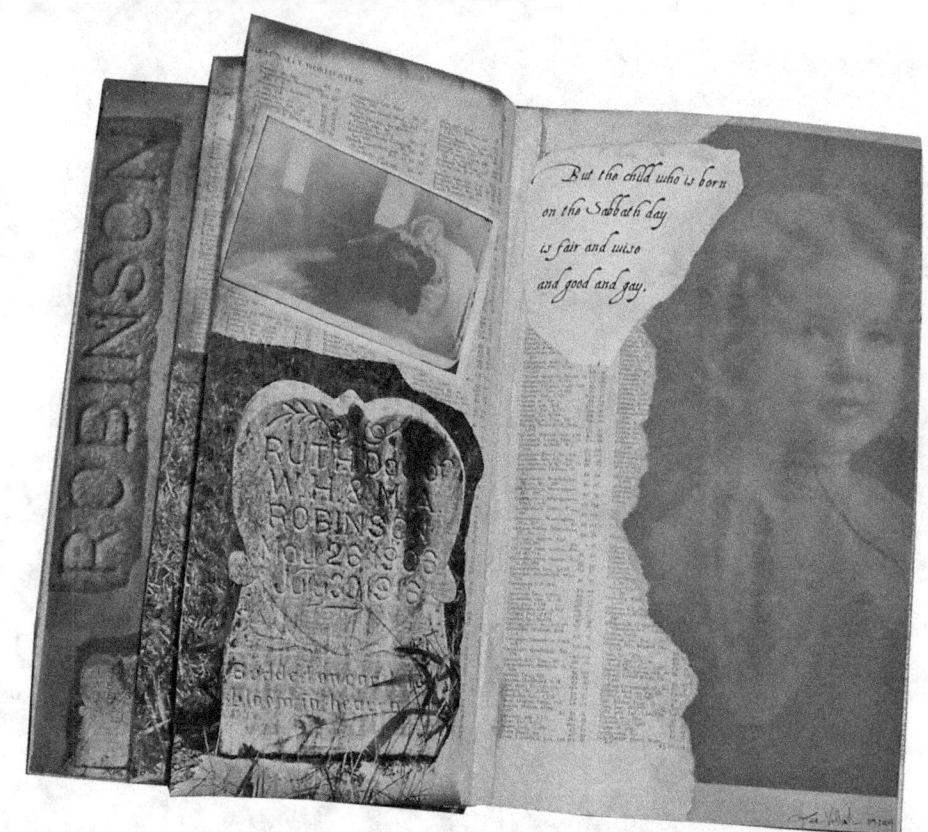

If I Had a Million Dollars...
My Obsession With The Woodmen's Circle Home

I occasionally receive emails asking about the very strange house that appears over and over again in my work. This is the story of that very sad house...

The Woodmen's Circle Home was built in 1929-1930 by the Supreme Forest Woodman Circle, an organization founded in 1892 as a ladies' auxiliary of the Woodmen of the World. Based on an idea put forth by Mrs. Talley Alexander, the estate was dedicated to providing a home for orphans and widows of members of the fraternal organization. Completed just as the country was struggling to deal with the Great Depression, the home provided a place for women and children who had nowhere else to go.

The original estate covered almost 240 acres, and cost over $150,000, most of which was sent by Woodmen of the World members around the country. In 1931, the Pennsylvania House was built on the grounds to house the orphans apart from the widows. Over 100 orphans passed through its doors between the 1930s and 1970s.

In the early 1970s, the estate was closed due to lack of code upgrades. One of the reasons cited was the lack of fire escapes. Ironically, the entire

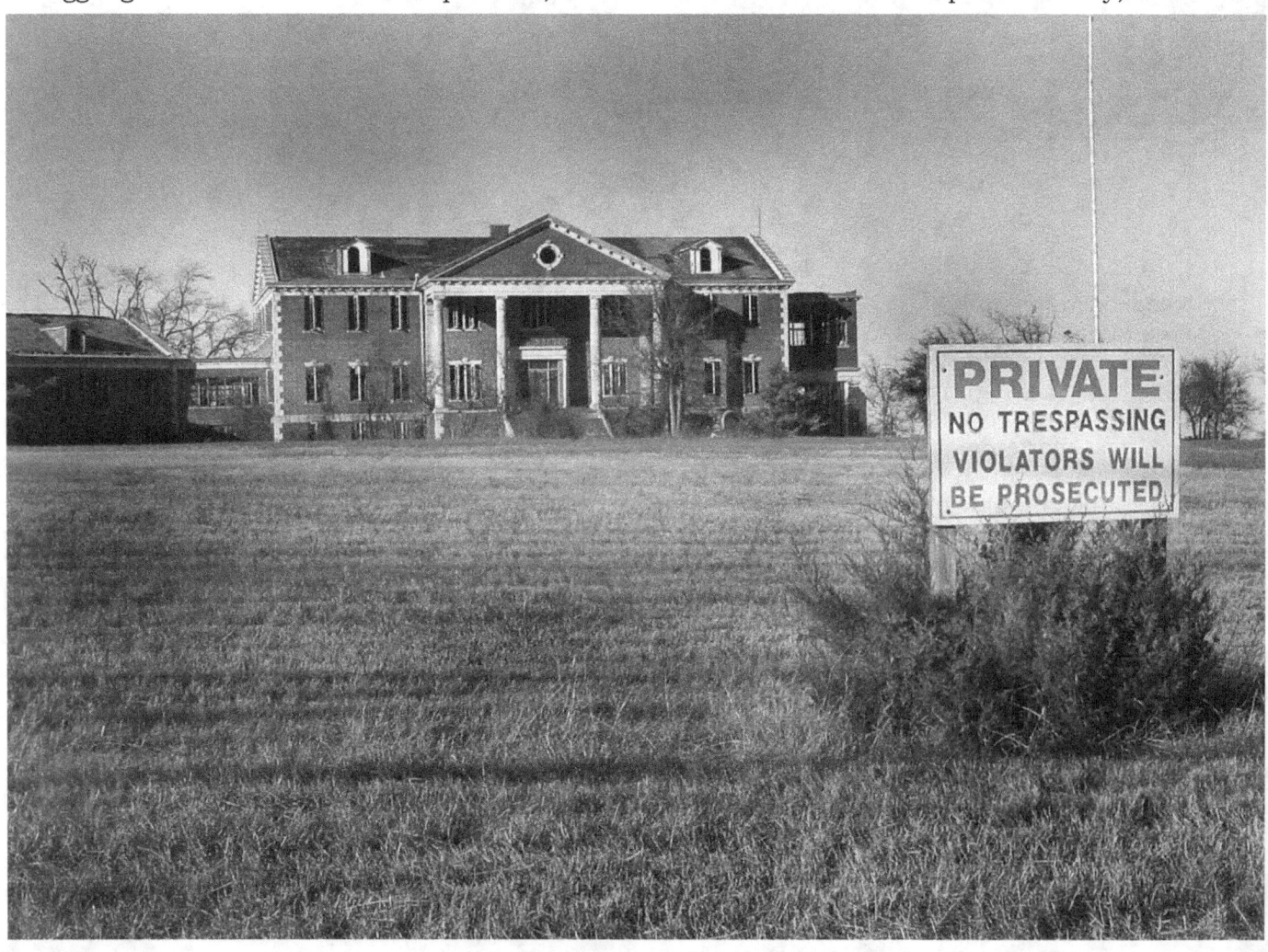

estate was burned by an arsonist in the 1990s, which partially accounts for its current poor condition.

Shortly after its closure, the estate was leased by a church. There are various local legends about the nature of the type of worship that went on in the building during. The church was ultimately forced to vacate after running up large debts with the City of Sherman.

In the 1980s, the estate was purchased by a group of local businessmen for an estimated $3.1 million dollars. It has changed hands several times since then, going from one savings and loan to another until it wound up in the hands of a local Sherman attorney. Although there have been constant rumors that the buildings will be restored and converted to some sort of hotel or business complex, there has been no activity on the grounds for well over a decade.

I first saw The Woodmen's Circle Home in 1994. I was living in Sherman, Texas, and a friend who had grown up in the area asked if I'd ever seen the haunted house on the edge of town. When I said no, we hopped in the car and took a ride. The moment I saw it, I was transfixed. In the middle of a large open field was a lovely red brick estate, clearly abandoned and beginning to decay. The windows were all broken out. The roof shingles were mostly gone, and there were places where the roof had fallen in. One outbuilding had no roof at all. Although the grounds around the estate had been mowed (it's illegal to leave property unmowed here, because of the fire hazard in the summer), there was scrub growing around the base of all the buildings. The trees were old, and mostly bare. This was truly the very picture of a Hollywood haunted house, out in the middle of nowhere.

Over a decade later, I still make regular trips up to Sherman to visit the house, usually with one or two photographer friends--- it's become quite a popular subject for photography here as it settles into serious decay.

The estate now occupies just 13 acres, but is still a formidable presence. It is sur-

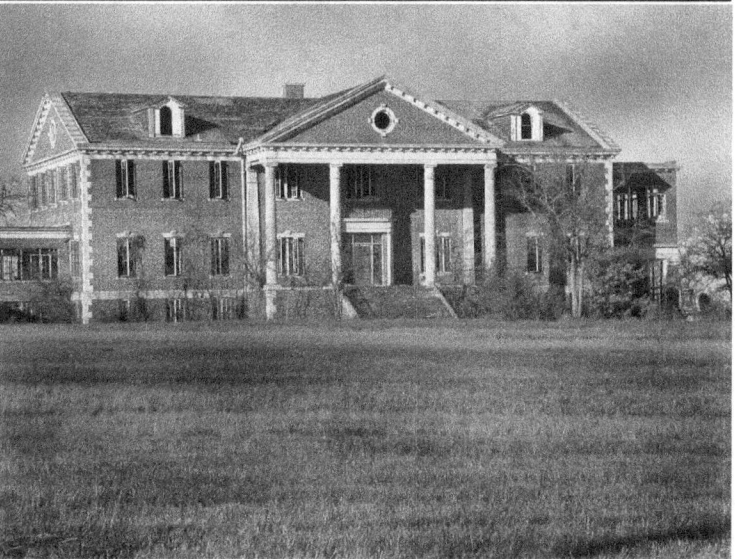

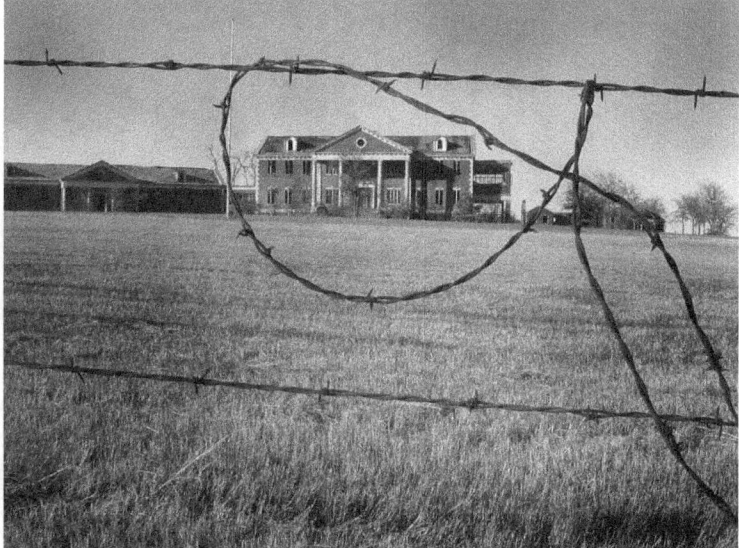

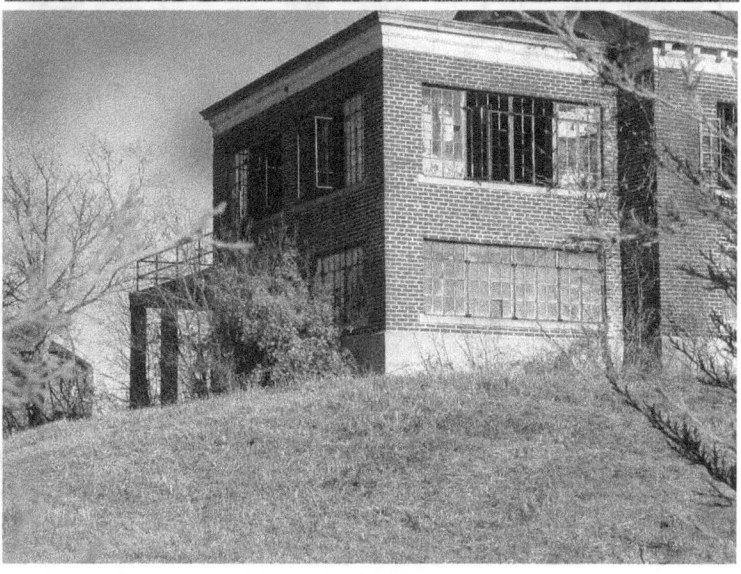

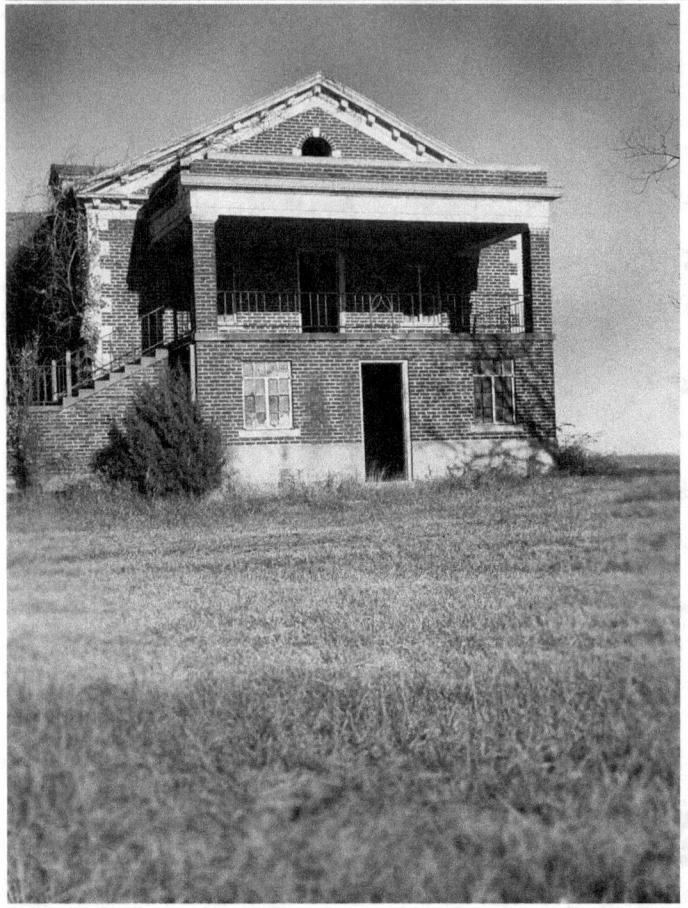

rounded by barbed wire, and clearly marked with signs not to enter, more for the protection of potential visitors than of the estate itself, There's really nothing left to break or steal, but the state of the floors and roofs makes it a dangerous place to explore. Although I've only photographed the buildings from the outside with zoom lenses, several photographers have applied for access and been taken inside, and their images show the severe case of decay inside.

I often dream of winning the lottery, and purchasing The Woodmen's Home. It really would make a lovely art retreat with a few million dollars worth of renovations. I've already set aside the side section of the main building, shown at left, with its wide second story porch, as my personal studio and residence. A girl can dream, can't she?

But then, renovation would mean all the local photography buffs would lose their favorite decaying subject. Perhaps it's best to let the house return to the earth on its own schedule.

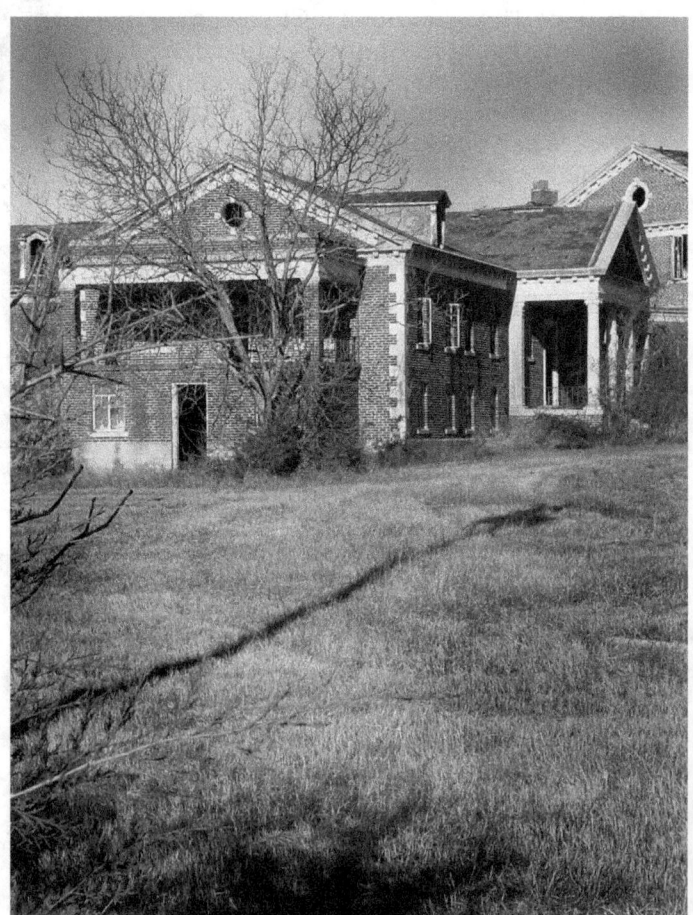

Do not stand on my grave and weep;
I am not there. I do not sleep.
I am a thousand winds that blow.
I am the diamond glints on snow.
I am the sunlight on ripened grain.
I am the gentle autumn's rain.
When you awaken in the morning's hush,
I am the swift uplifting rush
Of quiet birds in the circled flight.
I am the soft stars that shine at night.
Do not stand at my grave and cry;
I am not there. I did not die.

- Anonymous

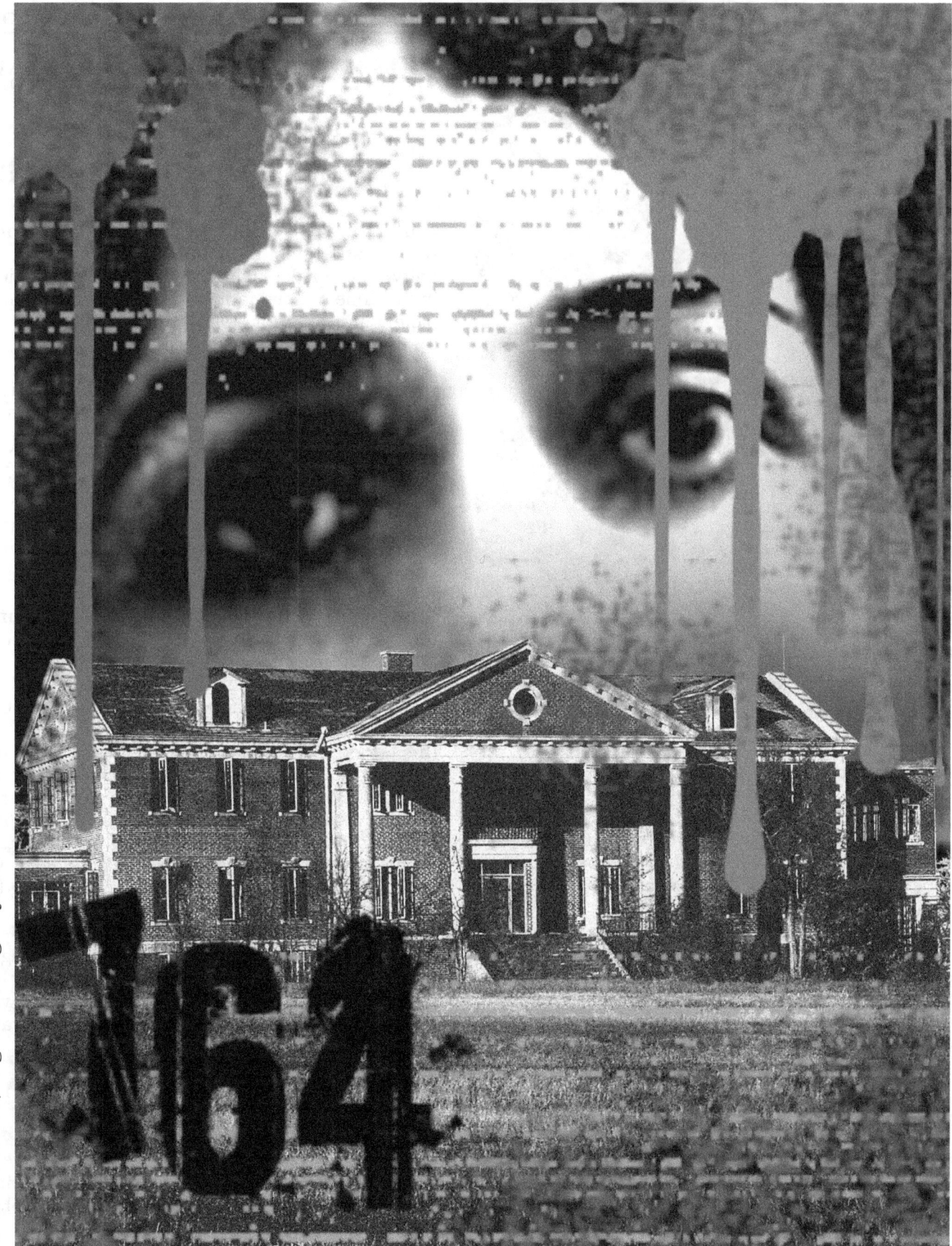

She Watches, digital collage by Lisa Vollrath

Dressing for Death
Mourning Dress
in Victorian Photographs

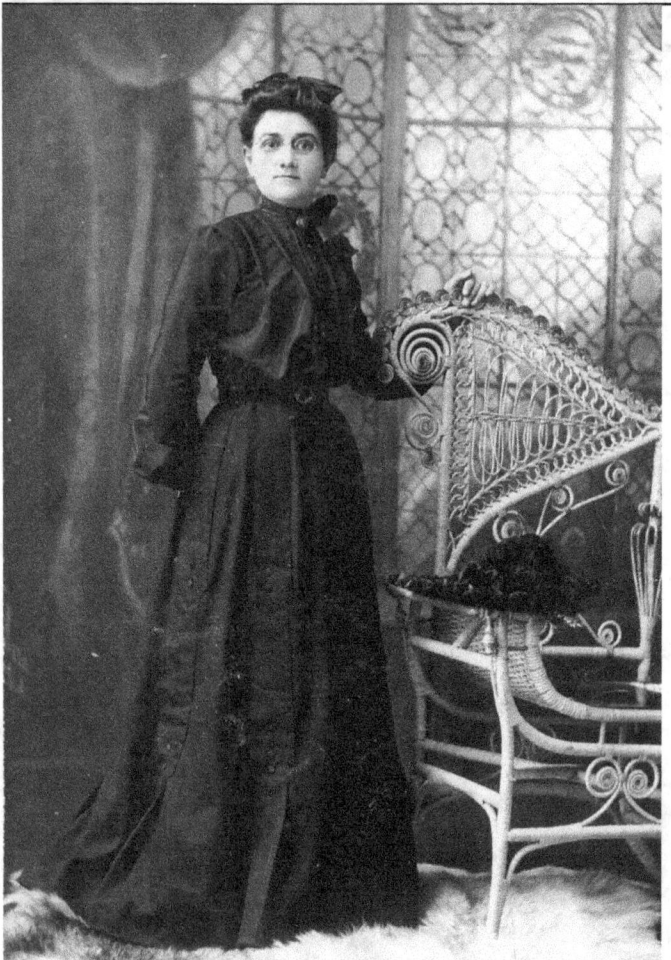

When her husband, Prince Albert, died of typhoid in November 1861, Queen Victoria went into full mourning for three years, and ushered in the Victorian cult of death. Victoria remained in mourning attire for forty years, until her own death in 1901, and Victorian society became positively obsessed with the whole idea of death and mourning.

Since child mortality rates were extremely high, and the average life expectancy was so short, mourning was a common experience in Victorian life. An elaborate set of rituals and rules dictated how family members should dress and behave for years after the death of a close relative.

The immediate family went into full mourning as soon as death was imminent. Mirrors were covered, clocks were stopped, and black clothing was worn. Wives and sisters went into seclusion.

Victorian society created strict rules for mourning attire, especially for women. Widows in particular were expected to follow a very stringent set of restrictions, both of dress and of social activity. These rules had the effect of isolating her in her time of need, and it was considered completely improper for a widow not to follow them upon the death of her husband.

To begin, a Victorian widow's mourning period lasted for over two years. The first period, considered full mourning, lasted for one year and one day. The widow would often remain completely secluded during this period, wearing only plain wool or crepe dresses devoid of any ornamentation. Other family members might venture out to church, their heads often covered in long weeping veils.

During the next nine months of second mourning, black lace and jewelry of black jet were permitted. Mourning jewelry was generally quite simple. Gloves made of silk or grenadine could now be worn. Attendance at serious social activities such as church could be resumed during this period. Long veils could be lifted and worn off the face. The photo of the woman above could be of a widow in this stage of mourning. Her dress is very plain, and she wears a very simple brooch at her neck. The hat sitting on the chaise to the right of her is plain black velvet. Older widows often remained in this stage of mourning for the remainder of their lives.

During the final six months of half mourning, a widow was permitted to wear demi-mourning colors of grey, white or mauve, generally mixed with black. Attendance at most social occasions was permitted.

Although there were mourning rules for men as well, they were much less restrictive. A man could return to his business as soon as he wished. If he was a widower, he might observe the two years of mourning, but it was left to his discretion when to end his observance, and also when to remarry.

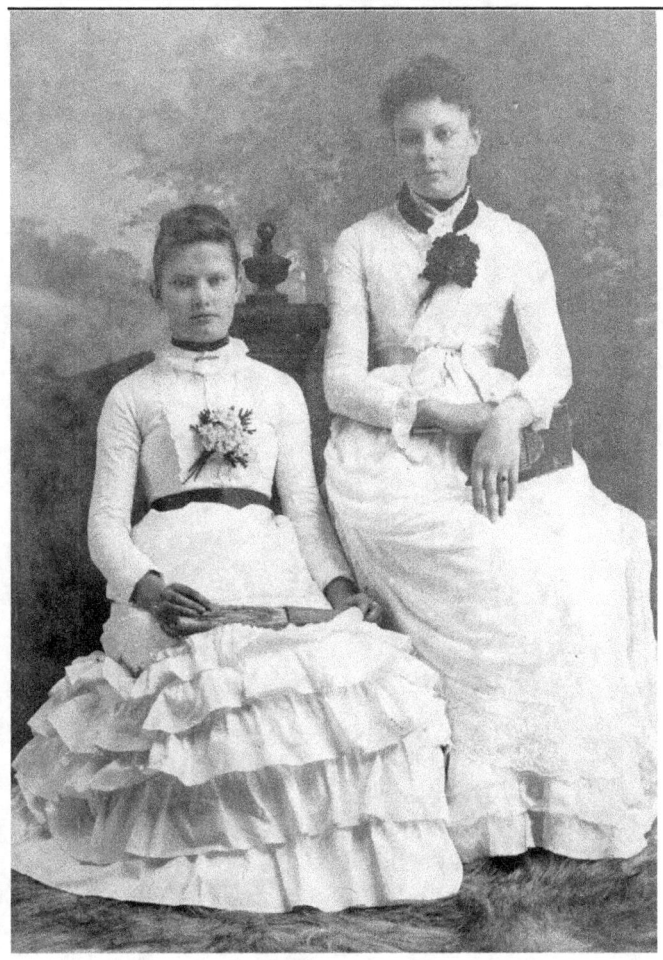

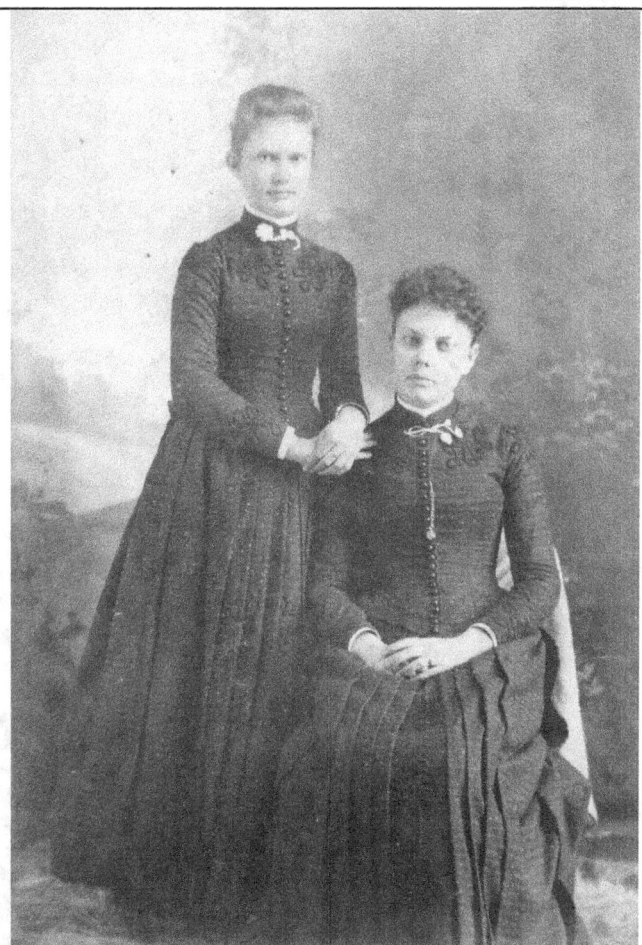

Mourning for parents was also somewhat strict.
Whether it was a case of parents marking the
passing of their children, or children mourning
the loss of their parents, it was standard to observe the a mourning period of one year and one
day. Six months were spent in full mourning,
three in second, and three in half mourning. An
example of half mourning can be seen on the
two sisters above. Although they are dressed in
white, the black trim on their dresses probably
indicates that someone in their family passed
away sometime in the last year or so.

It should be noted that these rules applied most
stringently to English women. In America, the
rules were relaxed somewhat, especially after the
Civil War. During this period, almost every
woman was in mourning for someone in her family, and when the war was over, society re-
sponded with a somewhat shorter and less restrictive mourning code. Simply put, people were
tired of seeing women constantly dressed in
black.

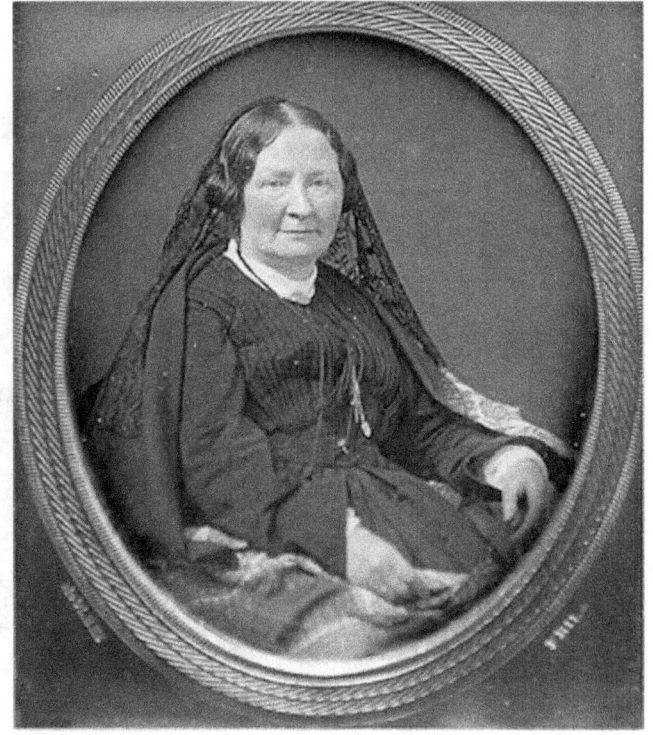

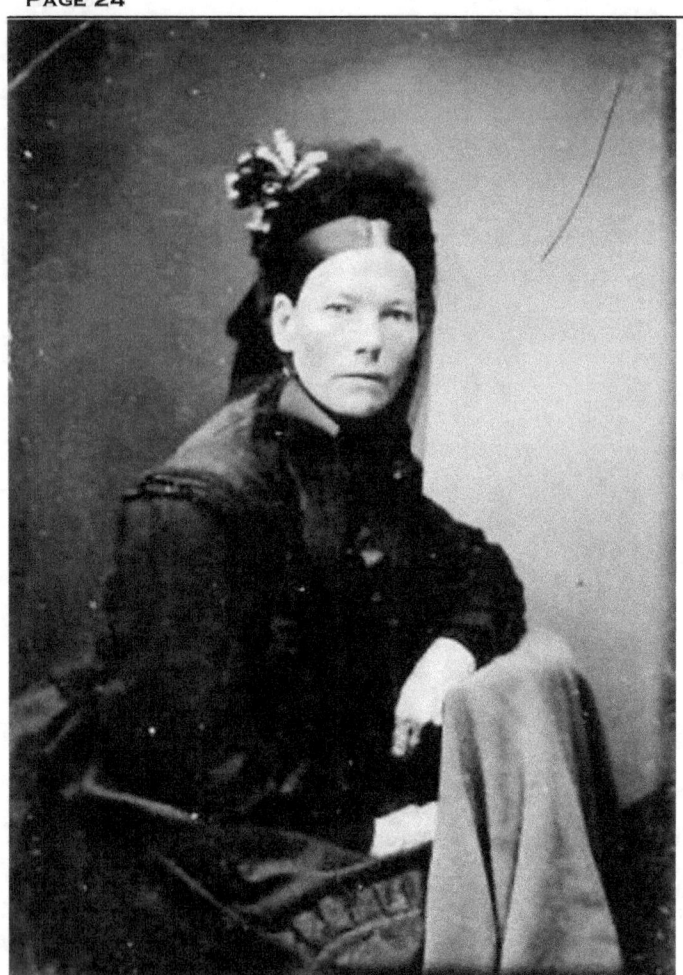

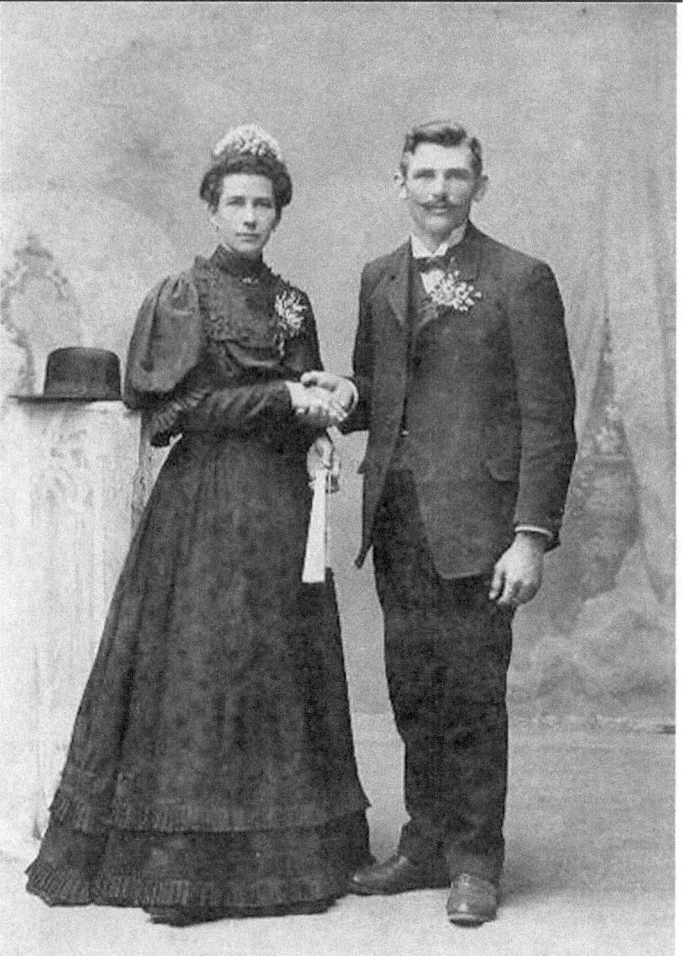

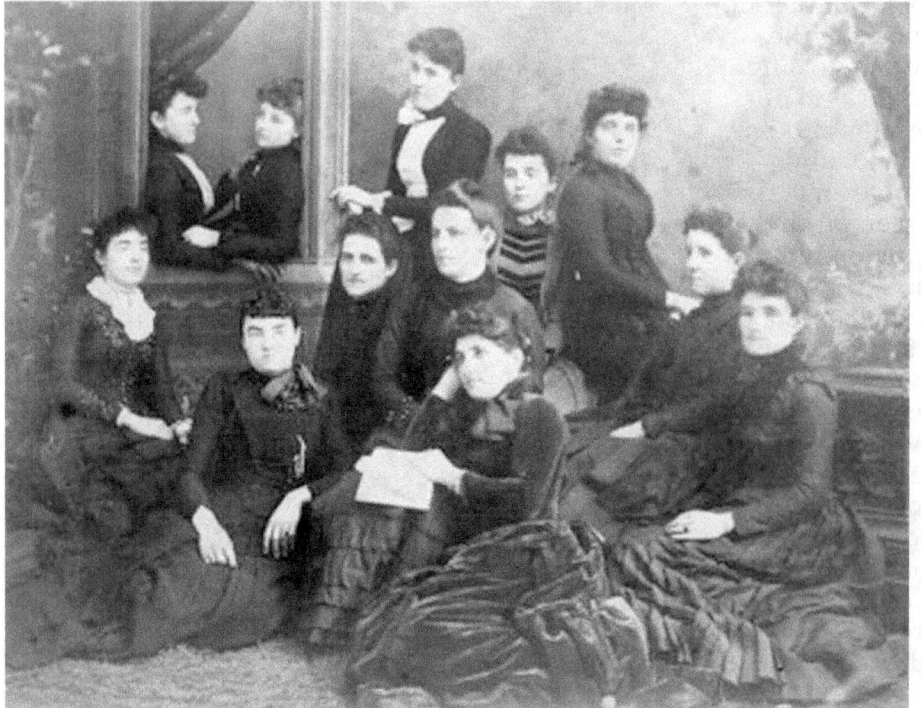

While we are
mourning the loss
of our friend,
others are rejoicing
to meet him
behind the veil.

- John Taylor

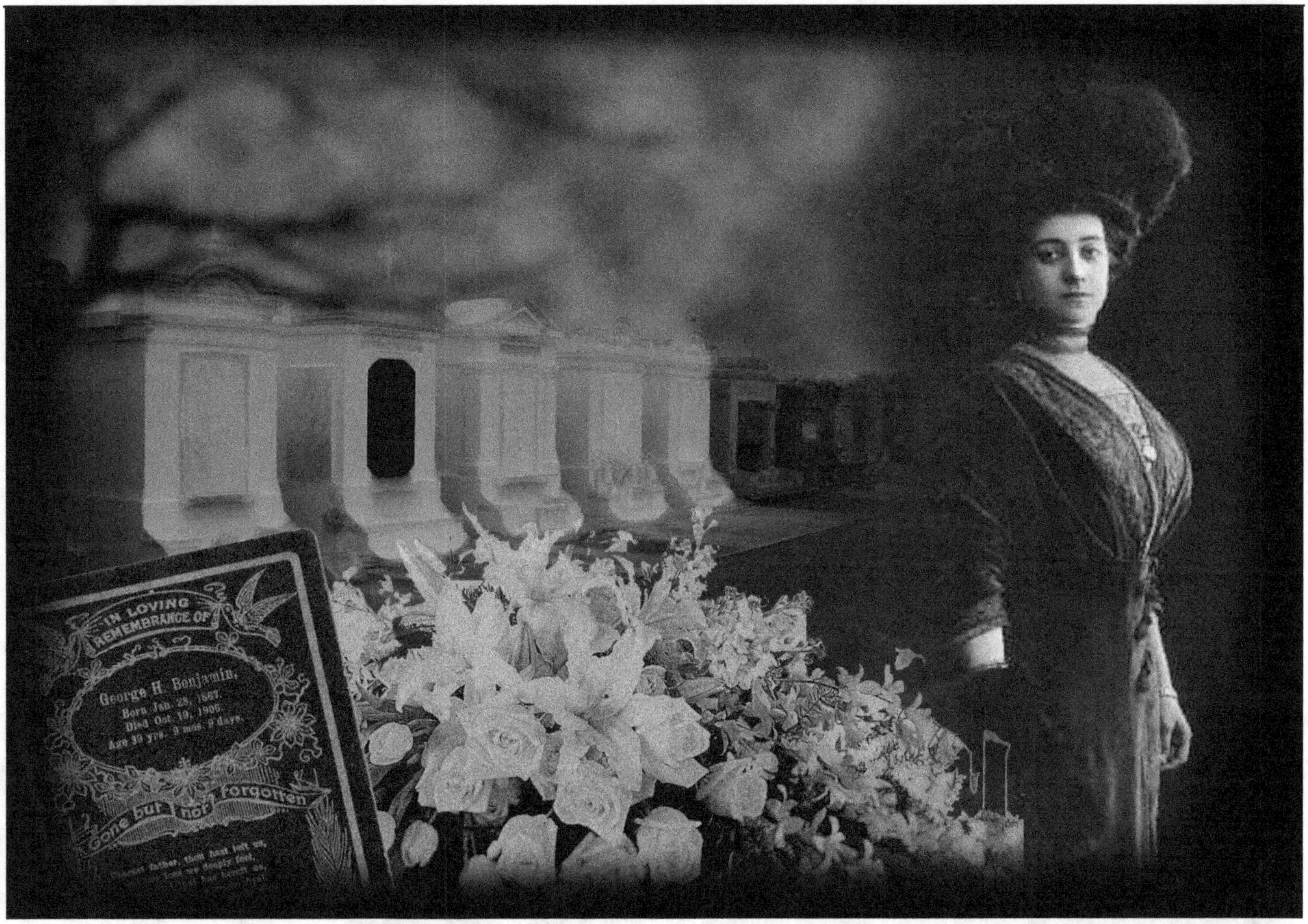

Gone But Not Forgotten by Lisa Vollrath

Notices & Disclaimers

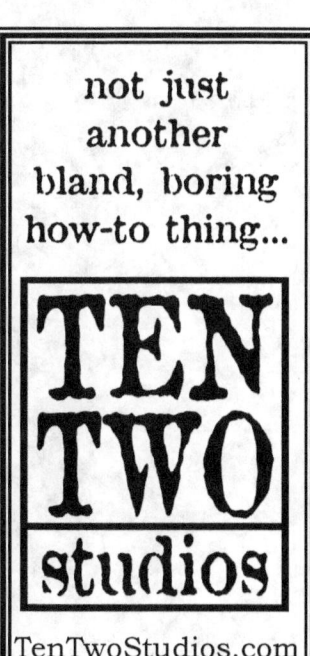

Someone to Watch Over Me
The Myth of Spirit Photography

The Victorian obsession with death created some interesting photographic anomalies. One highly collectible type of death-focused photos centers on spirits and visitors from the great beyond. These images, referred to as spirit photographs or ghost photographs, depict living, breathing subjects being visited by the dearly departed.

Early daguerreotypes and ambrotypes required their subjects to remain still for long periods of time while the plates were being exposed. Perhaps some early photographer realized that if a subject moved during the exposure time, the resulting image was blurred and somewhat transparent, as if a ghost had entered the photo. The first spirit photographs were created as novelties---simply a photographer showing off an interesting effect by adding ghosts to everyday scenes.

Strangely enough, a photographer named William H. Mumler began claiming in 1861 that his spirit photographs were the real thing. Mumler started a business as a sort of medium photogra-

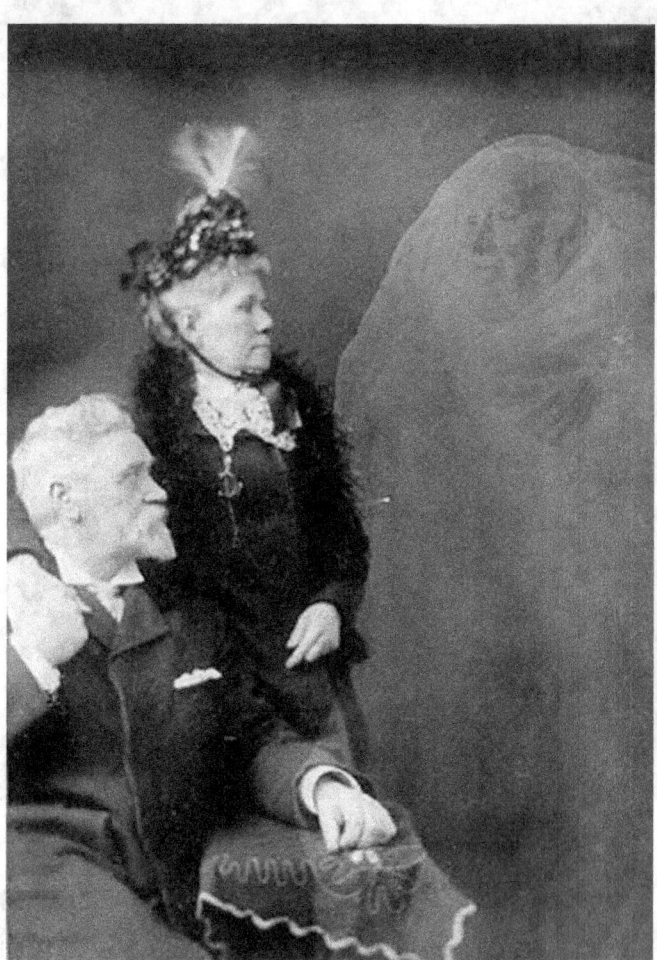

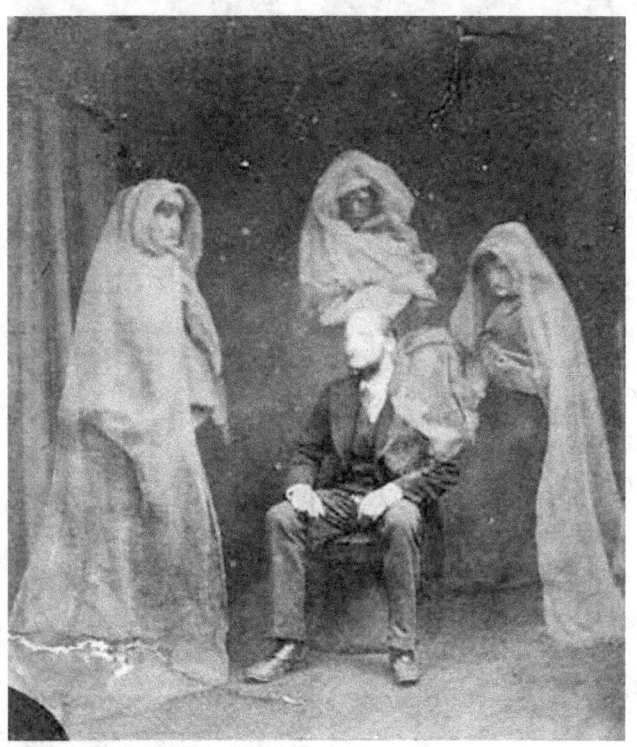

pher. He would photograph people in a normal studio setting, and the ghostly images of celebrities or relatives would magically appear on the negatives. For this service, Mumler charged ten dollars per portrait, while similar non-ghostly photos were available for just pennies. His photos set off an international obsession for spirit photography, and a scientific controversy about the photographing of spirits that continues to this day.

A modern viewer can easily see how these photos could be created as film techniques advanced, and exposure times lessened. As a very poor photographer myself, I've had the experience of double-exposing film---of taking a photo, forgetting to advance the frame, and taking another. The result is two images layered over each other. If my

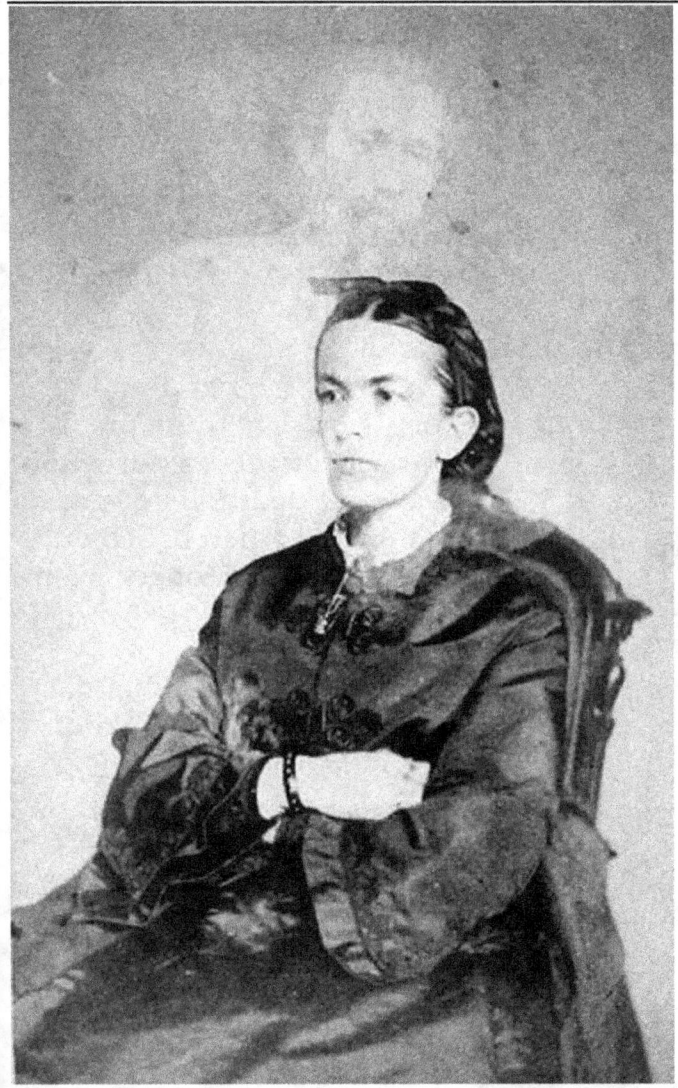

A photograph
is a secret
about a secret.
The more it tells you
the less you know.

- Diane Arbus

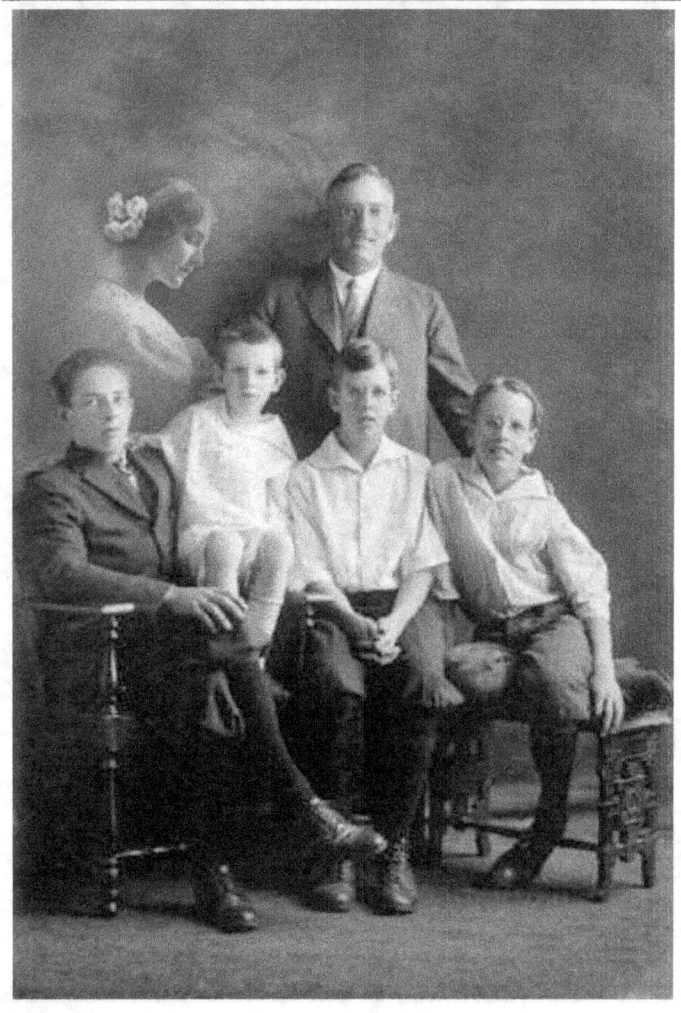

two subjects happened to be people, I'd have a very good facsimile of a spirit photograph.

Happily, we no longer have to rely on accidents or exposure times to create the illusion of spirit photographs. A few quick swipes of an eraser in PhotoShop, and a small adjustment in the opacity of layers, and the same effect is easily achieved.

On these pages are three "real" Victorian spirit photos, and two PhotoShopped fakes. Can you tell the difference?

(The photo above, and the two on the previous page are from the era. The photo to the right, and the one on the following page were created by yours truly on a computer---as was the artwork on page 29.)

Words for the Dead

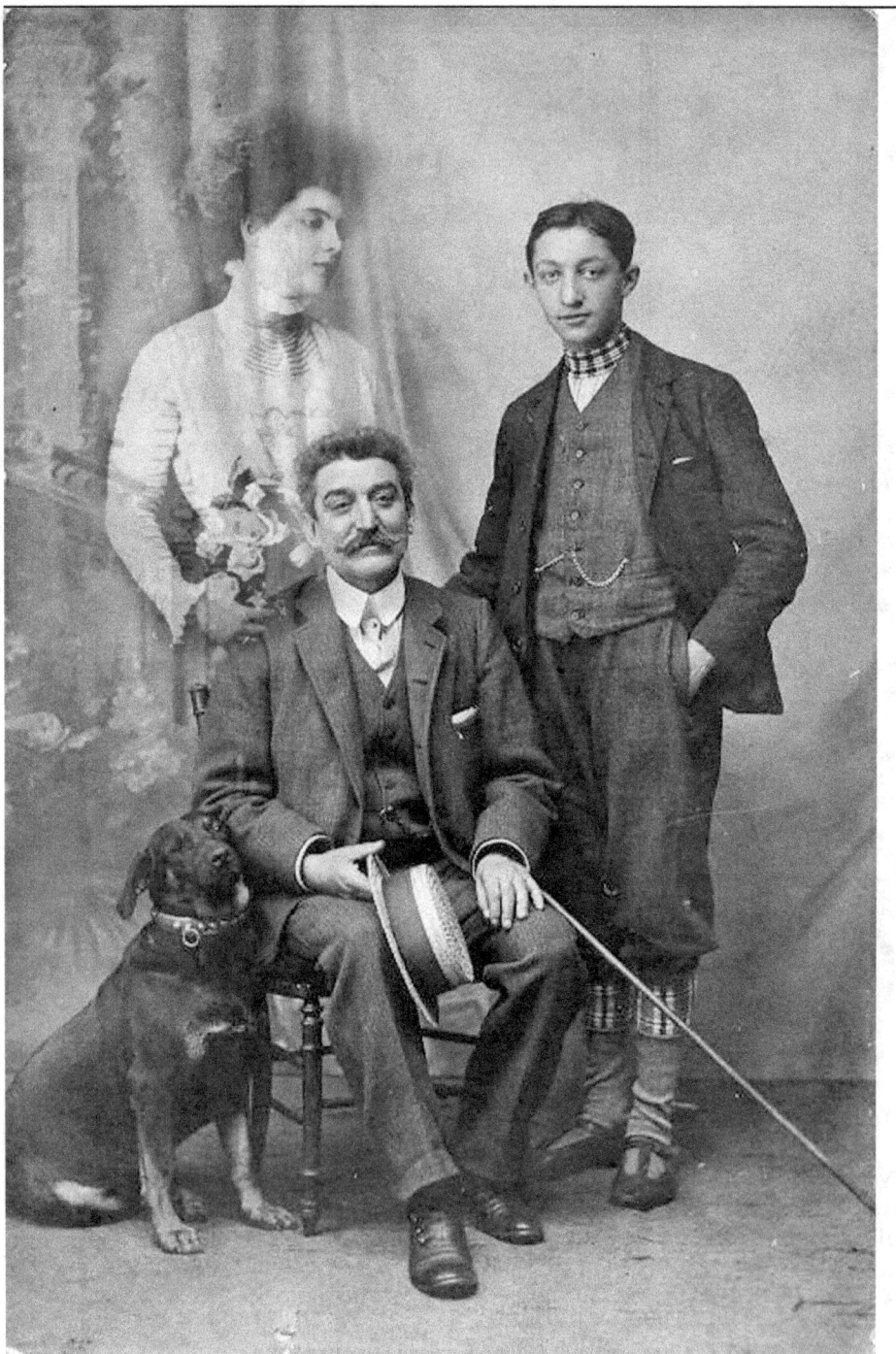

Death is a shadow that always follows the body.
--- 14th-century English proverb.

Death, the most dreaded of all evils, is therefore of no concern to us; for while we exist death is not present, and when death is present we no longer exist.
--- Epicurus

Death is the sound of distant thunder at a picnic.
--- W H Auden

Death lies on her like an untimely frost
Upon the sweetest flower of all the field.
--- William Shakespeare

Death is the veil which those who live call life:
They sleep—and it is lifted
--- Percy Bysshe Shelley

For death is no more than a turning of us over from time to eternity.
--- William Penn

While I thought that I was learning how to live, I have been learning how to die.
--- Leonardo da Vinci

Beside every dead person is a living ghost.
- Chinese proverb

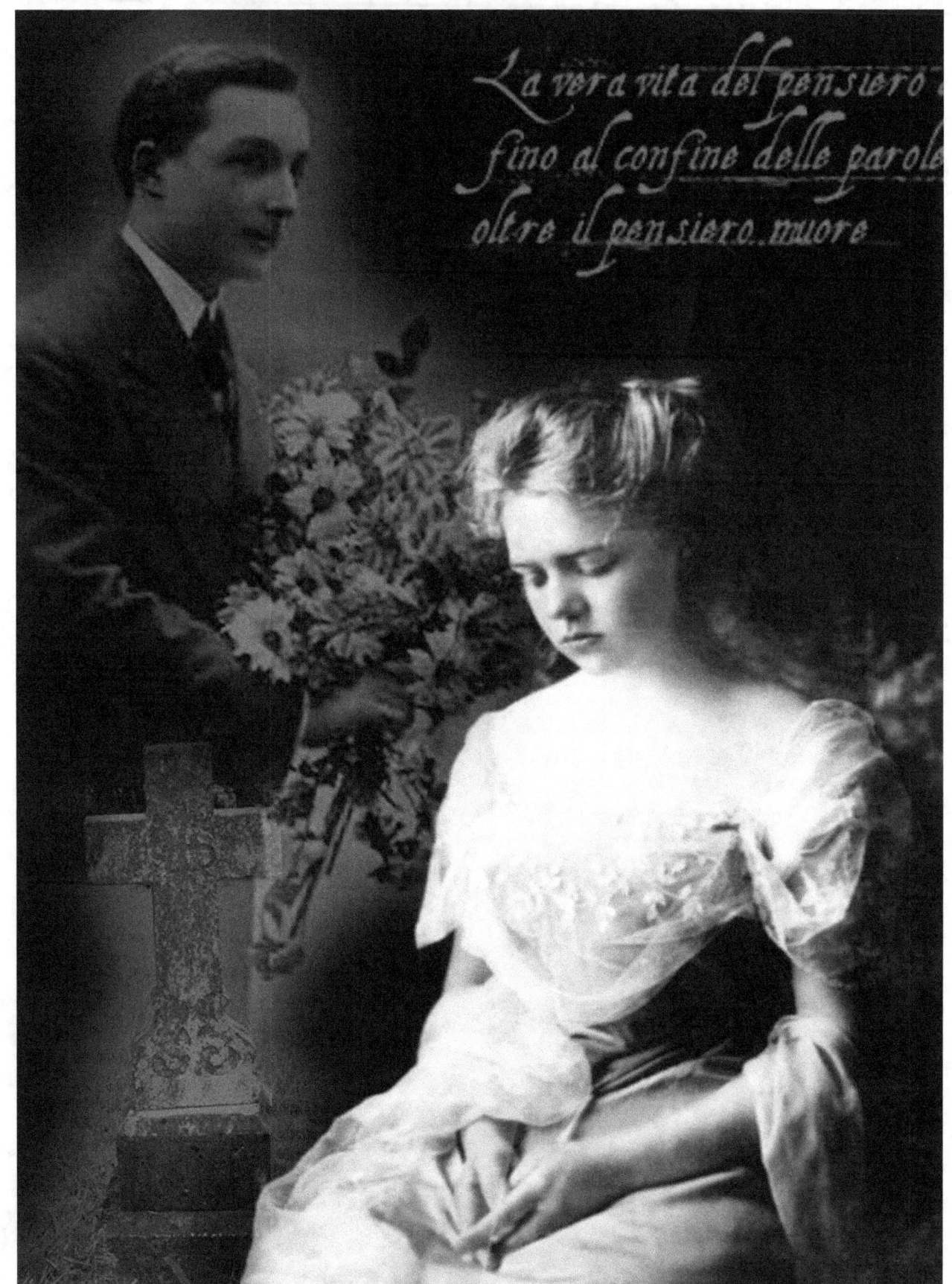

La vera vita del pensiero
fino al confine delle parole
oltre il pensiero muore

Everything Ends in Flowers, digital collage by Lisa Vollrath

www.ingramcontent.com/pod-product-compliance
Lightning Source LLC
Chambersburg PA
CBHW081246170526
45165CB00009B/3222